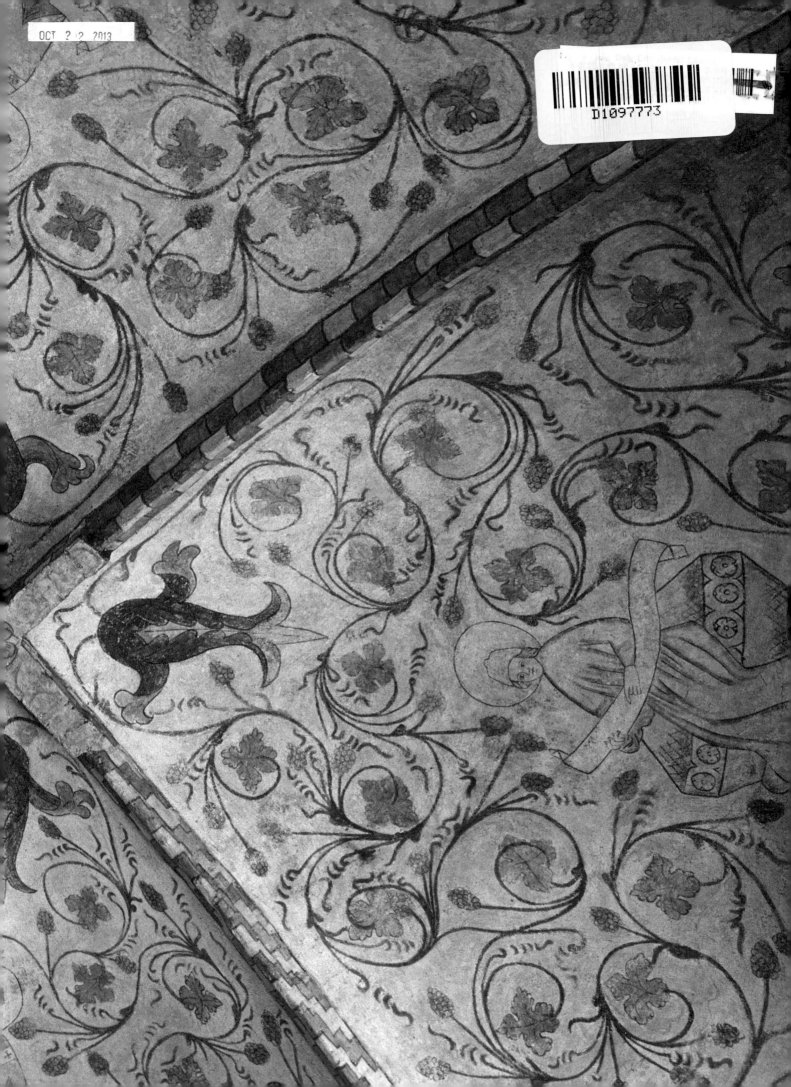

Medieval-Inspired Knits

Medieval-Inspired Knits

Stunning Brocade and Swirling Vine Patterns with Embellished Borders

Anna-Karin Lundberg

Trafalgar Square
North Pomfret, Vermont

W

Acknowledgements

I extend a big thank-you to everyone who helped make this book possible. Thank you to all the kind and very helpful church wardens who allowed us into the churches so we could look and be astonished as well as take photographs. Thank you to the photo models: Veronika, Lina, Herman, Erik, Axel and Mattias and the dog, Inga. Thank you to Kenneth for the lovely pictures of the photo models. Thank you to Eva Berg Hallberg and the government property office for allowing us to take photos in the exciting cloister room in the Östra Gymnasiehuset on Riddarholm in Stockholm. Thank you to Solbritt Benneth and Tina Rodhe at Museum of Medieval Stockholm for loaning us what we needed. Thank you to all the committed and encouraging people for support and advice: family, friends, neighbors, and all the friendly souls at the Historic Institute at Stockholm University. Thanks once more to everyone!

First published in the United States of America in 2012 by
Trafalgar Square Books
North Pomfret, Vermont 05053

Originally published in Swedish as *Maskor och Medeltid*

© 2012 Anna-Karin Lundberg, Tom Silvennoinen and Ica Book Publishers,
Forma Books AB

English translation © 2012 Trafalgar Square Books

ISBN: 978-1-57076-561-2

Library of Congress Control Number: 2012950746

Translation: Carol Huebscher Rhoades
Photography: Kenneth Ekelöv, Tom Silvennoinen
Proofreading/Copyediting: Eva-Lotta Staffas
Graphic Design: Collegit
Camera-ready copy: Linda Andersson
Editor: Susanne af Klercker

Printed in China

10 9 8 7 6 5 4 3 2 1

Table of Contents

Introduction

In 2005, by chance, I saw an incomparable treasure chest of motifs in the medieval churches in Sweden's Uppland province. Many of the churches are richly decorated with frescos utterly overflowing with luxuriant swirling vines, majestic stenciled patterns, graceful borders, and exciting color combinations. Besides embellishing and framing biblical scenes, painted decorations of various types were employed to emphasize the church interior's architecture, for example on the vault ribs, around the portals, and bowed windows. In the old Swedish peasant society, for centuries a person could draw inspiration from these interiors to apply to various types of decorative handwork: furniture making, wood carving and many textile techniques. In my case the inspiration from these fantastic decorative paintings led to a knitting project that I call Stitches and the Middle Ages. The result is this book: a collection of knitting patterns for unique hand knitted garments, where the painted embellishments have been transformed to contemporary knitting pleasure. A little bit of the Middle Ages to use for everyday – or more festive occasions – in our times.

Church Paintings

During the fifteenth century people began to install vaults in the Uppland church roofs and, in conjunction with this, decorated the walls and vaults with a rich assortment of frescos. The paintings I have been inspired by were made sometime

The richly painted interior in Sånga church. The paintings are from the third quarter of the fifteenth century; art historians consider the unknown artist as a member of the Tierp Group.

between 1450 and the early sixteenth century; in other words, during the Swedish Middle Ages. The technique used was called al secco, which means that the artist painted on a dry lime plaster using pigment blended with a binder. The color pigments were primarily minerals ground to powder and metals coated with verdigris until oxidized. Charcoal was used for black and lime for white. The artist could also use organic color materials. Examples of the different types of pigment are malachite and atacamite for green colors, azure for blue, iron oxide, cinnabar and red lead for different shades of red, lead tin for yellow, as well as ochre for the yellows and browns.

First the artist sketched the contours of the motif with charcoal on a plaster base. With delicate color sections, for example when painting the clothing of the figures, he cut into the lime so that the charcoal wouldn't blacken the color. After that he painted the motif with brushes of various sizes. Stencils were frequently used for painting borders, decorative motifs on the vaulted ceilings, backgrounds, and fine clothes with brocade-like patterns. The stencils were probably made with soft and flexible lead plate to make it easier to work on the uneven under layers that the churches' walls were often made of.

It wasn't the artist himself who freely chose which motifs would decorate the church interior. In large part, it was already determined by the church's mission to raise and educate the parishioners through depictions of the life and suffering of Jesus and the saints. They often used wood cuts as models; the best known example of such a model is the so-called Biblia pauperum – the poor people's Bible – which had been available since the thirteenth century. It consisted of 40 woodcut print

The paintings in Härkeberg church were made by Albertus Pictor in the 1480's and represent a prophet.

An example of how the colors in the paintings in Härkeberga church have changed. The sleeve painted on a foundation of wood is still a clear orange while the shoulder and collar that were painted on quicklime plaster are a noticeably darker shade.

pages where the Bible's stories are illustrated with two stories portending of the Old Testament for every New Testament motif. The Biblia pauperum was not a cheap edition of the Bible but was a picture Bible intended for the "poor in spirit," particularly aimed at parish priests so that they could better explain the biblical texts to their parishioners. In Sweden the 1460 edition became the dominant model for mural painting in the churches.

The paintings were made during the light and warm summer months and were probably finished within one season. During the winter half of the year the artist's studio – consisting of the painting master himself and one or two journeymen and apprentices – was probably occupied with other projects. For example, they might make preparatory sketches for the next project and other furnishing details for the church interior, such as the carvings and textiles. Albertus Pictor (or Albert the painter as he is sometimes called), who was also known under the name of Albert pearl knitter, is

the best known example of such comprehensive entrepreneurs for the church. Pearl knitting is an older word for embroidery and many artfully embroidered church textiles from Albert's studio are still preserved.

With time the paintings went through various changes. During the eighteenth century, literacy increased in the parishes and people read psalm books during the services. More light was then needed and therefore new windows were installed on the churches' previously closed north side, and, at the same time, small existing apertures were enlarged. As a consequence, some of the wall paintings were destroyed while the paintings on the vaults, for the most part, escaped unscathed. Many paintings were whitewashed over because of changed aesthetic ideals: clean white church interiors became desirable in line with neoclassical style. The nineteenth century interest in archeological research led to a renewed look at the old church frescos around the end of the century. The goal was to restore them which, among other things, meant filling in and improving. In some cases that led to covering the original so that it was almost unrecognizable. New standards for restoration were established during the early twentieth century, which held that fresco fragments should not be completed but simply preserved. In some cases they had to restore earlier restoration attempts.

Over the passage of time, the preserved wall paintings have become dirty, mostly due to the heating in the churches, but also because of soot flecks from living light and air pollution. Some color pigments have changed chemically to materials showing completely different colors, or have been bleached away by sunlight and acids in the air. For example, the face and hands are often a grey tone instead of pink, red cheeks have darkened, and clothing originally bright orange is now brown-purple. What we need today are diverse approaches so that we will know how to represent the paintings as they looked in their original colors.

Very few of the medieval painting masters are known by name now. The anonymous originators are usually divided into groups by painting style, and sometimes determined just by the ornamental art. I have divided the patterns in this book into three sections according to the school the original designers are considered to belong to: Albertus Pictor and his workshop (and the circle around him), the Mälar Valley School, and the Tierp Group.

It has been unbelievably fruitful for me to visit and study so many medieval churches while working on this book. These especially beautiful buildings, with their fascinating and imaginative paintings, have been preserved through the centuries for us. I only hope that we will continue to protect and preserve the old churches so that many future generations will have the opportunity to see them and wonder over their special beauty.

Early Knitting in Sweden

We know that knitting has been practiced in Europe since at least the middle of the fourteenth century. Paintings from that period show the Virgin Mary knitting a sweater in the round with four or five long double-pointed needles. In the sixteenth century, master knitters, primarily men, established guilds on the continent and made expensive luxury garments with fine silk yarns. In the same century, knitted silk garments, such as pattern-knit stockings, were imported for royalty and the nobility in Sweden. In the seventeenth century the importation of knitted garments increased, while at the same time, everyday clothing began to be knitted for people from all levels of society. We can't say much in particular about the latter because such simple clothing has not been preserved – it was used until it fell apart and then thrown away, although it is possible that the yarn was respun and recycled. One of the more luxurious garments from that period is a tulip patterned sweater knit with gold and silver threads and now preserved in the Nordic Museum's collection in Stockholm.

We don't know how or when knitting as handwork came to Sweden. Did it come from the British Isles, the Faroe Islands and Norway via Skåne and Halland (south and southwest Sweden) or from Germany by way of Visby, the Hansa city on the island of Gotland? In any case, the Uppland parishioners who lived during the Middle Ages didn't know how one knitted silk sweaters, and most of them probably never saw such a luxurious garment during their lifetime. But perhaps some of the church painters (whether native Swedes or from the continent) who came to the area had something like that in mind when they represented a Biblical person? I haven't found anything to support that theory, but it is an exciting idea to play with!

Colors, Materials, and Knitting Techniques

Colors are very important for my project. I have not tried to reproduce the original colors of the paintings but have mainly based my work on how they look today. Often a completely different and more richly colored shade shines forth from beneath an outer layer of darkened color, and that has sometimes influenced my color choice. The colors of the

garments have also been selected with respect to available yarn choices. It has never been my intention to directly replicate a motif as exactly as possible in stitches. In some cases it would have been impossible, in light of how knitting is structured. Instead, I have tried to capture a feeling of the color and form of the painting and combined those elements with one or more details from the motif.

I knit with a two-ply wool yarn spun in Sweden, which seems a natural choice considering the nature of the project. Wool is a historically proven, natural fiber with fantastic qualities: wool insulates even when wet, is relatively flame resistant and repels dirt. I have chosen a sportweight yarn and needles U.S. sizes 2-3 and 4 (3 and 3.5 mm) to ensure that the motifs are distinct. This results in a rather firm fabric that reminds me of traditional folk knitting. Because the garments in the book are knitted with a rather large number of stitches for the gauge, I recommend knitting a gauge swatch to make sure that your garment will be the right size. The swatch is very important if you normally knit loosely or if you are using another yarn than that recommended in the pattern. See the Technical Information at the back of the book for tips and ideas about how to make a gauge swatch in two-color stranded knitting.

Basically I use an old Nordic technique for two-color pattern knitting: knit on a circular needle (previously knitters used four or more long double-pointed needles) and never work with more than two colors at the same time. I use the Norwegian method for the armholes. I machine-stitch two lines from the shoulder to the underarm on each side of the seam line at the sides of the body and then cut the opening along the seam line. The advantage of this method is that the sweater body can be knitted on a circular needle in one piece from the bottom edge up and the armhole will be sized correctly for the finished width of the sleeve. To knit the body in the round up to the shoulder seam, I use the Fair Isle technique with neck "steeks" (adding extra stitches) that are then reinforced and cut open. The raw edge is folded under and sewn securely to the inside of the neck opening. A couple of garments in the book, such as the Härkeberga Golden Cloak, are made with steeks even for the armholes and have stitches picked up around each armhole for the sleeve, which is then knitted from the top down (making the stitches face downwards). In contrast to the other garments, you'll find a vest with sections knitted in a variation of intarsia (knitted with separate small skeins of yarn for each color section) combined with cable knitting. On a couple of models I've used simple embroidery to further highlight the pattern effect, while one scarf is lace knitting.

Most of the models in the book have simple shaping, which functions well with the traditional knitting techniques I use. It is also a way to emphasize the motifs, which are determined by the size of the sweaters. The motif for the Härkeberga Golden Cloak sweater is, for example, too big to be adjusted for more than one size. Some of the garments I have made are slightly figure formed at the waist with decreases and increases at each side of a solid colored side stitch. These garments have a basic square or a rounded armhole. One model, the Sånga Leaf pattern vest, has even borrowed its shaping from a medieval garment in a painting, but that is an exception.

These garments are a bit beyond the knitting abilities of a beginner but are easier to knit than you might at first think. It is not by chance that

earlier generations of knitters used these techniques to produce colorful and pattern-rich garments through the centuries. If you are unsure about your knitting capabilities but are drawn to knitting one of the patterns in this book, you can try out the techniques by knitting a smaller garment, such as a vest or child's sweater. If you've been knitting for a while and have made a few sweaters in two-color stranded knitting, perhaps you'll want to play and experiment with the pattern charts in the book to design a garment following your own taste and style. I recommend that all knitters explore their surroundings – the world around us is full of unexpected and useful motif treasures to be inspired by.

Knitting Instructions

Most of the knitting patterns in this book are designed for at least two sizes. The information for the larger size is listed within parentheses and, if there are three sizes, the largest two are within parentheses, separated by a comma. If only one number is given in the instructions, then it applies to all sizes. When knitting a pattern around on a circular needle or on double-pointed needles, the pattern chart should be read from right to left. When knitting a pattern in rows back and forth (turning at the end of every row), read the chart from right to

left for the right side rows and from left to right for the wrong side rows. The number of rows and stitches for a pattern repeat is shown on the chart with *--*; the repeat is repeated as many times as needed for the row or following information in the instructions. Note that it is not a given that the row ends with a complete pattern repeat, particularly for garments with a front opening and slits. If the row doesn't begin at the beginning of the repeat it will be noted on the chart.

Notions, such as buttons and clasps, that are required for some of the models, are listed at the beginning of the pattern. Common notions and tools that you might need besides the yarn and needles of various types and sizes are: stitch markers, a sewing machine, sewing thread and sewing needle, blunt tapestry needle (such as a blunt needlepoint needle), sharp scissors, pins, measuring tape, and steam iron. More detailed descriptions of the various techniques used for knitting the garments can be found in text and photos at the end of the book. You'll also find a list of abbreviations, there as well as information about the yarn the original garments were knitted with.

Note: Most of the garments were originally knitted with 2.5 and 3 mm needles. There is no exact U.S. equivalent for these sizes so we recommend that you either use metric sizes or the closest U.S. size that gives you the correct gauge.

Albertus Pictor

The originator of the paintings in Löt church is considered to have been someone in Albertus Pictor's circle of painters who possibly worked under the supervision of Albertus himself. This picture shows one of the roof vaults. Albertus often used the Biblia Pauperum as a model and his paintings in the pictured room are distinguished by more substantive figures with greater depth than those of earlier church painters. The garments in this section were inspired by the paintings in the Härke, Löt, and Bromma churches.

Lőt
Angel Wings Cardigan

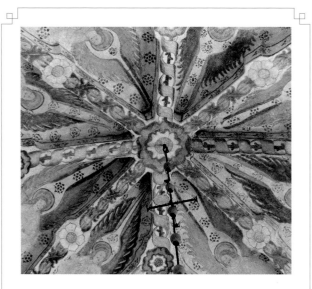

In one of the ceiling rosettes in one of the vaulted ceilings in Löt church, there are a multitude of painted angels. Their wings are folded in towards the center of the vault where the vault ribs meet, and they are surrounded by various stencil-painted, surface-filling motifs in iron oxide red. For some reason, the angels' bodies have been rubbed out, but their wings shift in a multitude of shades of, for example, verdigris green tones. The panels that decorate the cardigan Angel Wings have angel wings that meet, paired between narrower panels with small simple crowns inspired by the widespread stenciled motifs. The edges of the cardigan are decorated with a little motif inspired by a leafy vine that appears to grow out of one of the church's consecration crosses.

Cardigan

SIZES: M (L/XL)

FINISHED MEASUREMENTS:
Chest approx. 41 ¾ (48) in / 106 (114) cm
Length: approx. 23 ¾ (25 ¼) in / 60 (64) cm
Sleeve length: approx. 19 (19 ½) in / 48 (49.5) cm

YARN: Kampes 2-ply (100% wool; 328 yd / 300 m, 100 g) Sport or equivalent.

YARN AMOUNTS:
Black approx. 20 (20 g)
Malachite green 257 approx. 100 (120) g
Golden yellow 268 approx. 100 (120) g
Red-brown 204 approx. 110 (120) g
White (natural white) approx. 190 (230) g
Dark turquoise 250 approx. 60 (80) g
Light turquoise heather 251 approx. 90 (110) g

NEEDLES: U.S. sizes 1-2 and 2-3 / 2.5 and 3 mm: 16 and 32 in / 40 and 80 cm circulars + set of 4 or 5 dpn.

NOTIONS: 6 (7) pairs pewter clasps, approx. 1 ½ in / 4 cm long when closed.

GAUGE: 28 sts and 34 rows in pattern following chart B on larger needles = 4 x 4 in / 10 x 10 cm. Adjust needle sizes to obtain gauge if necessary.

KNITTING TIPS: Begin by reading completely through the instructions. Knit a gauge swatch to make sure you are working at the correct gauge. All of the single-color rows are worked with the smaller needles and the multicolor rows with the larger needles. The cardigan has facings around the plackets, neck, and front edges, so there will be a great deal of finishing as you sew down all the facings; however, it is well worth the effort.

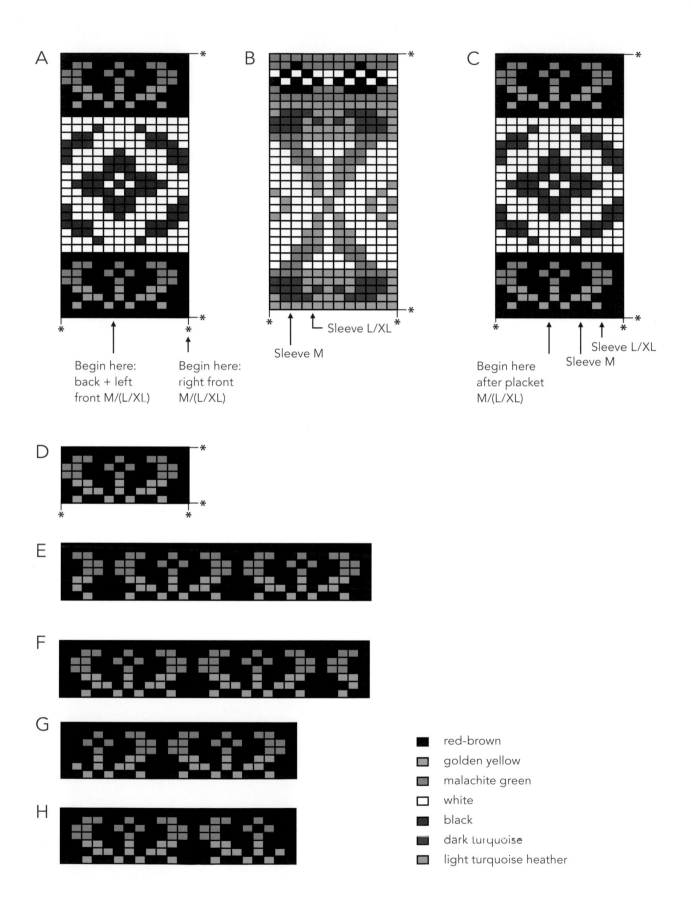

A

Begin here:
back + left
front M/(L/XL)

Begin here:
right front
M/(L/XL)

B

Sleeve M

Sleeve L/XL

C

Begin here
after placket
M/(L/XL)

Sleeve M

Sleeve L/XL

D

E

F

G

H

■ red-brown
■ golden yellow
■ malachite green
□ white
■ black
■ dark turquoise
■ light turquoise heather

BODY: With red-brown and long circular U.S. 1-2 / 2.5 mm, CO 299 (347) sts; join, being careful not to twist cast-on row. Place marker between last and first sts to indicate beginning of round. Knit 7 rnds in stockinette. The next rnd is the fold line and is worked as follows: K4, p66 (78), k8, p143 (167), k8, p66 (78), k4. Change to larger needles. On the next rnd, begin the pattern following chart A at arrow for your size. The first 4 sts of the round are the first half of the steek at center front and are knitted with alternating colors over the first 3 sts (checkerboard); the next st is an edge st and always knit with the MC. Work 66 (78) sts following chart A (= right front). The next 8 sts are the steek for the first side slit; the first and last sts in the steek are edge sts and knit with MC; the remaining sts in alternating colors (checkerboard fashion). Work 143, 167) sts following chart A (= back). The next 8 sts are a steek for the other side slit and worked as for the previous steek. Continue knitting following chart A to the last 4 sts (= left front), knit 1 edge st with MC and finish with 3 sts in alternating colors (checkerboard). Work in pattern following chart A for a total of 32 rnds. On the next rnd, BO side steeks (2 x 8 sts). Change to golden yellow and begin working pattern B. On the first rnd, CO 13 new sts over each gap above the bound-off sts of the side steeks. The round now has 309 (357) sts. Repeat the 32 rows of pattern repeat a total of 4 times, and then continue following pattern for another 8 (21) rnds. On the next rnd, BO the first 3 and last 3 sts on the round (the 6 sts of steek at center front); do not bind off the edge sts. Cut yarn. Place the steek edge sts together with the 14 sts to the left plus 14 sts to the right of the edge sts on a stitch holder (30 sts total). CO 4 new sts and work around, and end by casting on 4 sts = 281 (329) sts. The new front neck steek sts are worked as for previous steeks at center front. Continue knitting around in pattern following the chart and begin neck shaping: decrease 1 st on each side of the neck steek ssk to right of neck steek and k2tog on left) on every rnd 10 times, and then on every other rnd 4 times (= 14 sts decreased total). Work without decreasing for 7 rnds. On the next rnd, place the center 59 sts of back onto a holder. CO 8 new sts for a

steek for the back neck and finish the round. Begin shaping the back neck on the next rnd, decreasing 1 st on each side of the back neck steek. Decrease the same way on every other rnd another 3 times (= 4 decrease rnds total). Knit 1 more round. On the following rnd, BO all the steek sts as follows: BO 4 sts, work 44 (56) sts, BO 1 st (side st), work 44 (56) sts, BO 8, work 44 (56) sts, BO 1 (side st), work 44 (56) sts, BO the last 4 sts of rnd. Place each set of shoulder sts on a holder.

SLEEVES: With red-brown and smaller dpn, CO 61 (65) sts; join, being careful not to twist cast-on row. Knit 7 rnds for facing. Work foldline: p27 (29), k8, p26 (28). Begin working pattern as for body. Don't forget to work the single-color rnds with smaller needles and the two-color rnds with larger needles. Begin after the first st on of the rnd at the arrow for the sleeve on chart C. The first st is worked throughout with MC, the next 26 (28) sts following the chart, the next 8 sts are the sleeve slit steek and worked as for the body, and the rest of the rnd in pattern following the chart. After completing 8 rnds of chart C, begin shaping sleeve by increasing 2 sts at center of underarm on every 4th round (M1 after first and M1 after last st); work new sts into charted pattern. Knit a total of 24 rnds following chart C. Next rnd: BO the steek sts. On the next rnd, with red-brown, CO 13 new sts over the slit and then continue in pattern all around (except for the first st). After completing chart C, work following pattern on chart B. Continue increasing as before on every 4th round (change to circular when sts fit around). Work the 32-row repeat a total of 4 times and then continue in pattern for another 0 (5) rows. Continue with MC and smaller needles and knit 1 rnd and then purl 4 rnds for facing. On every purl rnd, increase 2 sts at center of underarm on every rnd (M1 after first st of rnd and M1 after last st). BO loosely.

FINISHING: Machine-stitch a line, beginning at the top and straight down all the steeks' 4th and 5th sts. Sew a vertical line of duplicate stitch with white yarn over the same sts on the steek for the opening at center front. Carefully cut the steek down the center, being careful not to cut into the stitch lines.

Lay a sleeve flat on a flat surface and measure the width immediately below the purl facing. Mark the corresponding armhole depth on each side of body by hand-sewing (with contrast color thread) straight down from the bound-off side st, beginning at top of armhole. Machine-stitch 2 lines on each side of the basting line and reinforce the side st at base of armhole with a couple of extra stitches to prevent stitches from running. Cut up between the machine-stitched lines. Using white (golden yellow) yarn, join the shoulders with three-needle bind-off (with RS facing RS) or join on RS with mattress st.

EDGINGS: As before, work the single-color rows with smaller needles and two-color rows with larger needles.
Neckband: With red-brown and smaller short circular, work the 15 sts on left side of center front holder, pick up and knit 31 sts along left side of front neck, pick up and knit 9 sts along right side of back neck, knit 59 sts from back holder; pick up and knit 9 sts along left side of back neck; pick up and knit 31 sts along right side of front neck, knit 15 sts from right side of front holder = 169 sts total. Change to larger circular and work in pattern following chart D for 7 rows; the first row is WS. After completing chart D, cut MC and continue in red-brown, purling 1 row on RS for the foldline and then work in stockinette for 7 rows. BO loosely.
Slits on Body: Pick up the sts for the edging on the body slit to the right of the slit working from the top down up to and including the foldline of facing, to the left of the slit going up from the foldline. With RS facing, red-brown and smaller needles, pick up and knit 29 sts and work back and forth in pattern following charts E (right side) and F (left side) for 7 rows. The first row is a WS row. When charted rows are done, cut MC and purl 1 row on RS for foldline. Continue in stockinette for 7 rows and then BO loosely.
Sleeve slits: With red-brown, smaller needles, and RS facing, pick up and knit 22 sts and work in pattern following chart G (right side) and H (left side) as for slit on body.
Front bands: The sts for the band on right front are picked up from the bottom up, from the foldline of the facing and up to the foldline of neck, to the left front's front edge from the foldline of neck and down. With red-brown and smaller needles, pick up and knit 145 (157) sts and work in pattern following chart D, as for slits.

Sew the cut front edge steek to the wrong side with small loose stitches. Overcast the other steek edges on the WS. Fold in the edgings, beginning with the bottom edge, then the front edges and finally the neck. Sew them down with small loose stitches on the WS using red-brown yarn. Sew the edging of each slit invisibly with small stitches slanting upwards on the slit. Attach sleeves, fold in facings over the cut edges and sew securely to inside with small loose stitches. Weave in all ends. Gently steam press the sweater under a damp pressing cloth. Sew on the clasps centered on the six (seven) topmost motifs on the front edges (see photo).

Löt
Saint's Floor Jacket

Saints Barbara and Katarina of Alexandria are pictured on one of the walls in Löt Church. They are standing on a floor patterned with geometric shapes painted in strong colors. Just below that is a checkerboard painted panel that also appears in several other Uppland medieval churches. The floor and the black and white pattern from the panel have inspired the Saint's Floor cardigan, which has somewhat heavier edgings and a collar in patterned garter stitch.

Jacket

SIZES: S/M (M/L)

FINISHED MEASUREMENTS:
Chest approx. 39 ¾ (43) in / 101 (109) cm
Length: approx. 23 ¾ (24 ½) in / 60 (62.5) cm
Sleeve length: approx. 19 (19 ¾) in / 48 (50) cm

YARN: Kampes 2-ply (100% wool; 328 yd / 300 m, 100 g) Sport or equivalent.

YARN AMOUNTS:
Black approx. 30 (40 g)
White (natural white) approx. 50 (50) g
Red-brown 204 approx. 250 (280) g
Golden yellow 268 approx. 100 (110) g
Light yellow 209 approx. 140 (160) g

NEEDLES: U.S. sizes 1-2 and 2-3 / 2.5 and 3 mm: 16 and 32 in / 40 and 80 cm circulars + set of 4 or 5 dpn.

NOTIONS: 2 (3) buckles and straps (for example a kilt buckle), a piece of rep woven band approx. 1 ¼ in / 3.5 cm wide and 4 in / 10 cm long. *Note:* You might need 3 buckles to close the larger size jacket at the front.

GAUGE: 28 sts and 32 rows in pattern following chart B on larger needles = 4 x 4 in / 10 x 10 cm. Adjust needle sizes to obtain gauge if necessary.

KNITTING TIPS: Begin by reading completely through the instructions. Knit a gauge swatch to make sure you are working at the correct gauge. *Two-color garter stitch:* When working garter stitch in the round, alternate knit and purl rounds. Always float the unused color on the wrong side (WS). When knitting back and forth, knit all rows and hold the stranded yarn in front when working on the WS so that all the floats stay on the WS (inside of garment).

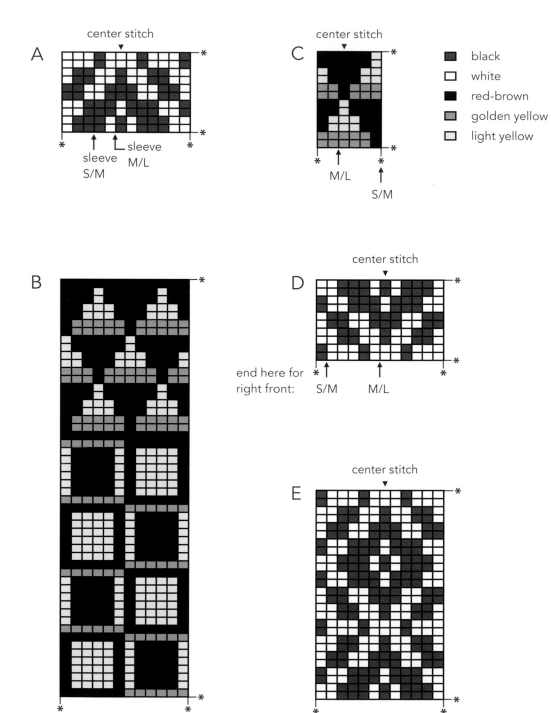

center stitch

A

sleeve
S/M

sleeve
M/L

center stitch

C

M/L

S/M

black
white
red-brown
golden yellow
light yellow

B

center stitch

D

end here for
right front:

S/M

M/L

center stitch

E

~ 22 ~

BODY: With white and smaller circular, CO 279 (303) sts. Do not join; change to larger circular and work back and forth in two-color garter stitch following chart A (except for the first and last sts which are always knit with white as edge sts) for 10 rows. Cut black, change to smaller circular and knit 2 rows with white. Note: On the second row, decrease 1 st at the center of the row. Cut yarn and change to red-brown. CO 3 new sts and work the row in stockinette, ending by casting on 3 new sts. The 6 new sts + the first and last (edge) sts are now the steek at center front. Work the 8 steek sts as follows: always knit the first and last sts of the steek with red-brown; alternate colors for the remaining sts checkerboard fashion. Change to larger circular, place marker between the last and first sts of the rnd to indicate beginning of rnd and work around in pattern following chart B. Work the 52-row pattern repeat a total of 2 times and then work in pattern for another 52 (50) rows. Next rnd: BO 3 sts (= last 3 sts of steek), knit 1 edge st, knit the rest of the rnd up to the right side of the steek, knit 1 edge st and then BO the remaining 3 sts of steek; cut yarn. Place the left edge st and 11 sts to the left of the edge st on a holder. With red-brown, CO 4 sts and continue in the round to the right edge st; place it and the last 11 sts of row on a holder and then CO 4 sts. The 8 new sts are for the front neck steek which is worked as for the center front steek (1 edge st, 6 checkboard sts, 1 edge st). Continue in the round following the chart and decreasing 1 st on each side of the neck (with k2tog on right side of neck and ssk on left) on every rnd 6 times and the on every other rnd 3 times. Now work 13 rnds without decreasing. Finish by working 1 knit rnd with red-brown as follows: BO 4 sts, work 92 (104) sts, place the next 52 sts on a holder for back neck, work 92 (104) sts and then BO 4 sts. Divide the shoulder sts and place 46 (52) sts each on 4 separate holders for shoulders.

SLEEVES: With white and smaller dpn, CO 68 (72) sts. Change to larger dpn and join to work in the round following pattern on chart A for 10 rnds; begin at arrow for your sleeve size. Cut black and continue with white and smaller dpn: knit 1 rnd, purl 1 rnd. Next rnd: change to larger dpn and work pattern following chart C, beginning after the first st of the rnd at the arrow for the sleeve; always knit the first stitch of the round with red-brown throughout. On every 4th rnd, increase 2 sts centered on the underarm: M1 after the first st and M1 after the last st; always work new sts into charted pattern. Work the 12-row pattern a total of 12 (13) times and then continue in pattern for another 6 (0) times (change to circular when sleeve is big enough). The sleeve should now be approx. 19 (19 ¾) in / 48 (50) cm long. Continue with red-brown and smaller circular: knit 1 rnd and then purl 4 rnds for the facing. On the purl rnds, increase 1 st on each side of the first st of the rnd. BO loosely.

FINISHING: Machine-stitch straight down between the front neck steek's 4th and 5th sts, beginning at the top. With red-brown sew a a vertical line of duplicate sts over the same stitches. Cut the steek open down the center. Reinforce the center front steek the same way.

Lay one sleeve flat on a flat surface. Measure the top width of the sleeve immediately below the purl facing rows and mark the corresponding armhole depth on the body by sewing, with contrast color thread, a basting line straight down and centered at the side between two sts. Machine-stitch 2 lines on each side of the basting line and reinforce with a couple of extra stitches at the bottom edge of the armhole. Cut open at the center between the stitching lines, in the thread between 2 sts. Be careful not to cut into the stitching lines because the stitches can unravel. Join shoulders with three-needle bind-off (with RS facing RS) or graft with Kitchener stitch on RS using red-brown yarn.

Right front band: With white, smaller needles, and RS facing, pick up and knit 121 (128) sts along the right front edge, beginning at lower edge. Knit 1 row on WS. Change to larger needles and work in 2-color garter st back and forth following chart D: see arrow for front edges where the row ends. The first and last sts (edge sts) are always knit with white. Work in pattern for 10 rows; cut black. Change to smaller needles and knit 1 row. On the next row, BO knitwise on WS. Work the left front band to correspond to the right band, but pick up and knit sts beginning at the neck and work down. Work the chart mirror-image.

Collar: With white, smaller needles, and WS facing, place onto needle 120 sts from the inside of the neck opening (WS) as follows: pick up and knit 12 sts from the left front holder, 22 sts along the left front side, 52 sts from the center back holder, 22 sts along the right side front, and 12 sts from the right front holder. Turn and knit 1 row and, at the same time, increase 1 st (M1) at the center of the row = 121 sts. Change to larger needles and work back and forth in two-color garter stitch pattern following collar chart E; the first and last sts are always knit with white as edge sts. After completing charted rows, change back to smaller needles and knit 1 row. On the next (WS) row, BO knitwise.

Tack down the steek on the WS with small loose stitches. Attach sleeves, folding the facing over the cut edges and then sew down on inside of body with small loose stitches. Weave in all ends on WS. Lightly steam press the sweater (except for garter stitch sections) under a damp pressing cloth. Sew a piece of rep woven band as reinforcement at the top under the right front edge. Sew on the buckle straps over the woven band (towards the underside of the front edge) and then sew the buckles to the left front.

Härkeberga
Twisted Leaf Panel

In Härkeberga church some of the vault ribs are decorated with painted leafy garlands that twist around a long, felled branch. I've used this motif for the front of the Twisted Leaf sweater. The twisted leaf panel has garlands on both sides of small groups of multi-lobed leaves (the same leaf motif that I used for the Little Leaf sweater). The leaf panels and the leaves are emphasized by simple embroidery in lighter colors. The sides, back, and sleeves have a small and closely repeated partial motif from a stencilled decoration on the same vault.

Sweater

SIZES: M (L)

FINISHED MEASUREMENTS:
Chest approx. 46 ½ (50 ½) in / 118 (128) cm
Length: approx. 26 ½ (27 ½ in / 67 (70) cm
Sleeve length: approx. 19 ¾ (19 ¾) in / 50 (50) cm

YARN: Kampes 2-ply (100% wool; 328 yd / 300 m, 100 g) Sport or equivalent.

YARN AMOUNTS:
Dark red-brown 253 approx. 320 (360) g
Light turquoise 244 approx. 330 (370) g
Small amounts of dark gold 266 and white (natural white)

NEEDLES: U.S. sizes 1-2 and 2-3 / 2.5 and 3 mm: 16 and 32 in / 40 and 80 cm circulars + set of 4 or 5 dpn.

NOTIONS: 6 round brass buttons, approx. ¾ in / 1.8 mm diameter.

GAUGE: 28 sts and 32 rows in pattern following chart B on larger needles = 4 x 4 in / 10 x 10 cm. Adjust needle sizes to obtain gauge if necessary.

KNITTING TIPS: Begin by reading completely through the instructions. Knit a gauge swatch to make sure you are working at the correct gauge.

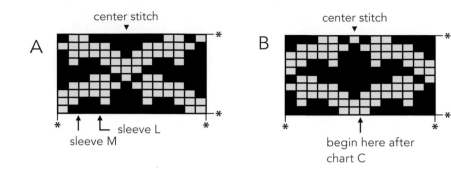

A — center stitch ▾

B — center stitch ▾

* sleeve L
* sleeve M

begin here after chart C

- ■ dark red-brown
- ☐ light turquoise
- ▨ knit with light turquoise and embroider with duplicate stitch in dark gold
- ⊟ knit with light turquoise and embroider along top edge with back stitch and white
- ▣ knit with dark red-brown and embroider along top edge with back stitch and white

BODY: With dark red-brown and long smaller size circular, CO 316 (340) sts; join, making sure that the cast-on row is not twisted. Place a marker between the first and last stitch to indicate beginning of rnd. Begin working in two-color k2, p2 rib. Work the knit sts with dark red-brown and the purl sts with light turquoise. Work in rib for 2 ¾ in / 7 cm. Now work 1 rnd in stockinette with light turquoise and, at the same time, increase 20 (24) sts evenly spaced around = 336 (364) sts. Change to larger circular and work in pattern following chart A (B) over the first 57 (64) sts and then chart C over the next 55 sts. Note: Size L: begin chart C on row 31 (see note on the chart). Next, work chart A (B, see note on chart) over remaining sts on rnd, beginning at the arrow for your size.

Work a total of 180 (190) rnds in pattern = 4 complete (10 rnds + 4 complete) repeats in length from the pattern repeat on chart C, plus another 20 rnds in pattern. On the next rnd: work 67 (74) sts, place the next 35 sts on a holder for the front neck. CO 8 sts for the front neck steek and continue working in the round. The steek sts are worked with alternating colors checkerboard fashion. Note: The steek does not have edge sts. Begin shaping the neck on the next rnd: decrease 1 st (with k2tog on right side of neck and ssk on left) on each side of the steek on every rnd 18 times. All decreases are worked with turquoise. On the same rnd as the 12th decrease, place the center 59 sts of the back on a holder for the back neck. CO 8 sts for a back neck steek and work as for front neck steek. Continue in the round and decrease 1 st on each side of the back neck steek on every rnd 6 times.

Work the next rnd as follows: BO 2 sts, work 47 (54) sts, BO 10 sts (the steek + the decreased sts), work 47 (54) sts, BO 3 sts, work 47 (54) sts, BO 10 sts (steek + decreased sts), work 47 (54) sts, BO 1 st. Place each set of shoulder sts on a holder.

SLEEVES: With dark red-brown and smaller dpn, CO 56 (60) sts. Divide the sts evenly over the dpn and join, being careful not to twist cast-on row. Work around in two-color rib as for body for 2 ½ in / 6 cm. With light turquoise, knit 1 rnd, increasing 20 sts evenly spaced around = 76 (80) sts total. Change to larger dpn and work in pattern following chart A, beginning after the first st of the rnd at the arrow for the sleeve; the first st of the rnd is always knit with light turquoise. Increase 2 sts at the center of the underarm (M1 after the first st of the rnd and M1 after the last st) on every 4th rnd. Work new sts into pattern following the chart (change to a circular when there are enough sts to fit around). When the sleeve is 19 ¾ in / 50 cm long, or desired length, cut dark red-brown. With light turquoise and smaller circular, knit 1 rnd and then purl 4 rnds for the facing. On the purl rnds, increase 2 sts centered at underarm: M1 after the first st of the rnd and M1 after the last st. BO loosely.

FINISHING: Machine-stitch a line through the center of each of the 4th and 5th sts in the neck steeks. Sew a vertical row of duplicate st over the same steek sts. Cut the steeks up the center between the duplicate st lines, avoiding cutting in the stitches. Lay a sleeve flat on a flat surface and measure the sleeve's width immediately below the purl facing rows. Mark the corresponding armhole depth on

C

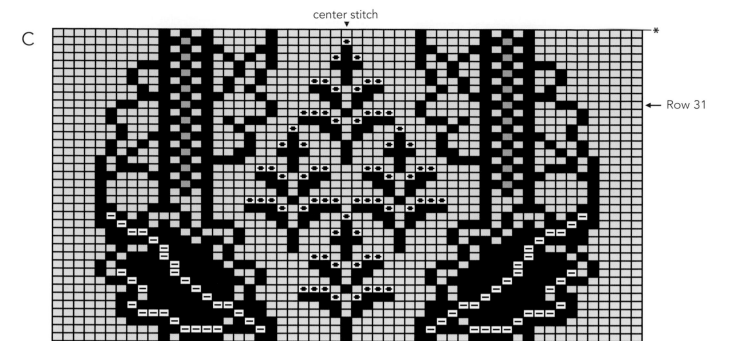

← Row 31

the sides of the body by hand sewing, with contrast color thread, straight down from the bound-off side st. Note: Subtract approx. ⅝ in / 1.5 cm from the width of the sleeve at the top of the armhole for the ribbed edge that will be buttoned over the shoulders (this will be added later). Machine-stitch 2 lines on each side of the basting lines and reinforce the side stitch at the base of the armhole with a couple of stitches so that the stitches won't run. Cut the armhole open through the center of the center stitches and down between the machine-stitched lines, being careful not to cut through the stitch lines.

With light turquoise and smaller needles, pick up and knit stitches for the top ribbed edging, beginning at the back: 47 (54) sts from right back shoulder, 8 (7) sts along right side of back neck (picking up in the row with decreased sts), 29 sts from back stitch holder, M1, work the remaining 30 sts from back holder, 8 (7) sts along left side of neck (in row with decreased sts), 47 (54) sts from left back shoulder = 170 (182) sts total. Turn and begin working in two-color rib as before but now work back and forth on RS and WS. Make sure that all the floats are on WS. Begin and end the row with 2 dark red-brown sts (knit these sts on RS and purl them on WS). Work in ribbing for 8 rows, cut light turquoise, work 1 row ribbing with

k2, p2 and dark red-brown. Next row: BO in ribbing. Ribbed front band: with light turquoise and smaller needles, work 47 (54) sts from left front shoulder, pick up and knit 20 (19) sts along right side of front neck (pick up in row with decreased sts), work 17 sts from front stitch holder, M1, work 18 sts from front stitch holder, pick up and knit 20 (19) sts at left side of neck (in row with decreased sts), work 47 (54) sts from right front shoulder. Turn and work in ribbing as for back ribbed band for 4 rows. Next row: Work 6 (8) sts, BO 4 sts – all binding off for buttonholes is made with stitches in alternating colors: * work 12 (14) sts, BO 4 sts; repeat from * once (= 3 buttonholes), work 86 sts, *BO 4 sts, work 12 (14) sts; rep from * once, BO 4 sts, work 6 (8) sts. On the following row, CO 4 sts over each gap. Continue in rib for 2 more rows. Cut light turquoise and work 1 row in rib with k2, p2 with dark red-brown. Next row: BO in ribbing. Lay the short ends of the front ribbed band over the back ribbed band and sew with a couple of stitches, so the armhole is complete. Attach sleeves; fold facings down over cut ends and sew down by hand on inside of body. Weave in all ends. Embroider over the center panel at the front following chart C. Lightly steam press (except for ribbing) under a damp pressing cloth.

Sew on buttons on back shoulder ribbing.

Härkeberga
Golden Cloak Sweater

Sweater

SIZE: M/L
FINISHED MEASUREMENTS:
Chest approx. 48 in / 122 cm
Length: approx. 24 ¾ in / 63 cm
Sleeve length: approx. 19 ¼ in / 49 cm
YARN: Kampes 2-ply (100% wool; 328 yd / 300 m,
100 g) Sport or equivalent.
YARN AMOUNTS:
Black approx. 310 g
Dark old gold 203 approx. 70 g
Old gold 266 approx. 150 g
Light orange 267 approx. 80 g
Golden yellow 268 approx. 50 g
NEEDLES: U.S. sizes 1-2 and 2-3 / 2.5 and 3 mm: 16
and 32 in / 40 and 80 cm circulars + set of 4 or 5
dpn.
GAUGE: 28 sts and 32 rows in pattern following
chart A on larger needles = 4 x 4 in / 10 x 10 cm.
Adjust needle sizes to obtain gauge if necessary.
KNITTING TIPS: Begin by reading completely through
the instructions. Knit a gauge swatch to make sure
you are working at the correct gauge. The garter
stitch edgings are worked on the RS with knit and
purl stitches. Make sure that the floats always stay
on the WS (inside of garment) when changing colors, even when working purl stitches. The stitches
for the sleeves are picked up around the armhole
and worked from the top down. *Note:* Due to the
size of the motif, this sweater is designed for one
size only.

This painted scene in the Härkeberga
church shows the three wise men vis-
iting Mary and the Baby Jesus. The
scenes from this wall are damaged but the
brocade pattern in gold on a black background is still clear. The decorative pattern
on Mary's cloak inspired the Golden Cloak
sweater. The checkerboard patterned bands
are made in the same shades as for the brocade pattern. The motif and the combination
of subdued and glowing colors transform
this sweater into a very special garment!

center stitch ▼

A

center stitch ▼

B

*

sleeve

- ■ black
- ■ dark old gold
- ■ old gold
- ■ light orange
- □ golden yellow

BODY: With larger circular and black, CO 336 sts. Join, being careful not to twist cast-on row; place marker between last and first st of rnd to indicate beginning of round. Begin with the checkerboard lower edge following the instructions below. Make sure that you always hold the colors on the WS when twisting them to change colors.

Rnd 1: *K2 with black, k2 with dark old gold; rep from * around.

Rnd 2: *P2 with black, p2 with dark old gold; rep from * around.

Rnd 3: *K2 with old gold, k2 with black; rep from * around.

Rnd 4: *P2 with old gold, p2 with black; rep from * around.

Rnds 5 and 6: Work as for Rnds 1-2, substituting light orange for dark old gold.

Rnds 7-8: Work as for Rnds 3 and 4, substituting light golden yellow for dark old gold.

Now work Rnds 5 and 6; 3 and 4; 1 and 2. Finish with 1 knit round in black. Next, work the pattern following chart A. Work the 76 rows of pattern repeat once and then continue in pattern for another 31 rnds = 107 rnds of pattern knitting. Cut yarn. Begin armhole steek: place the first 2 sts of rnd and last st on a holder. CO 4 new sts and work 165 sts following the chart; place the 3 following sts on a holder, CO 8 sts and work to end of rnd; CO 4 sts. The rnd now begins at the center of the steek for the left armhole. The first and last sts of the steeks are always worked with black (= edge sts to use when picking up sts for each sleeve); the other 6 sts should be worked in alternating colors (checkerboard). Continue in charted pattern for another 61 rnds. Front neck: On the next rnd, place the center 45 sts of front on a holder. CO 8 new sts for a front neck steek and continue working in the round. The first and last sts of the steek are always knitted with black; the rest alternating colors checkerboard fashion. Decrease 1 st on each side of the steek (with k2tog to right of steek and ssk to left) on every rnd 7 times. Then decrease 1 st at each side on every other round 3 times. On the same round as the 7th decrease, place the center 57 sts on back on a holder. CO 8 sts for a back neck steek as for the front and decrease 1 st on each side of the steek on every other rnd 4 times. Continue without shaping for 6 rnds. With black, knit and, at the same time, bind off the first 4 sts of the rnd, work 50 sts, BO 8 sts (front neck steek), work 50 sts, BO 8 sts, work 50 sts, BO 8 sts (back neck steek), work 50 sts, BO last 4 sts of rnd. Place each set of shoulder sts on a separate holder.

SLEEVES: Hand-stitch a row of back stitches beginning at the top and down through all the steek's 2nd and 7th sts (the sts nearest the black edge sts). Be careful to stitch through all the stitches in the line. Cut steek open with sharp scissors between the two center stitches. Seam shoulders with Kitchener stitch for an invisible join or, with RS facing RS, join with three-needle bind-off.

With black and short, larger size circular, pick up and knit the center and left st of the 3 sts on the left sleeve's stitch holder, pick up and knit 137 sts evenly spaced around the armhole's black edge sts, knit the last st from stitch holder = 140 sts total. Work around in pattern following chart B, beginning after the first stitch of the round at the marker for the sleeve; the first st of the round (centered at underarm) should always be knit with black. On every 4th rnd, decrease 1 st on each side of the black center underarm st with k2tog at the beginning of the round and ssk at the end. Change to dpn when stitches no fit around circular. After 34 decreases work another 4 rnds without shaping = 139 pattern rows. Continue without shaping and knit 1 rnd with black. Change to smaller dpn and work checkerboard pattern as for the body. BO (not too loosely) with black. Work the right sleeve as for the left.

FINISHING: With black and short, smaller size circular, pick up and knit 13 sts along right side of back neck, work 57 sts from back neck, pick up and knit 13 sts along left side of back neck, 18 sts at right side of front neck, work 45 sts of front neck, pick up and knit 18 sts at left side of front neck = 164 sts total. Work the neckband following the instructions for the lower edge of the body, beginning on Rnd 7. When the checkerboard pattern is complete, BO with black.

Trim the steeks to a 3-st width including the edge st. Sew down the edge with a line of half cross stitch, beginning at the bottom edge, towards inside of sweater. Make sure that the stitches catch any floats on the front and back. Next, working top down, sew the other half of the cross stitches. Sew loosely! If you pull in the stitches too tightly, you risk that the edge will be like a hard ridge on the inside of the sweater. Weave in all ends. Lightly steam press sweater under a damp pressing cloth but do not press the checkerboard edges.

Härkeberga
Flowery Vine Vest

A wonderful swirling flower vine that inspired this Flower Vine vest is painted on a vault rib in the Härkeberga church, just to the right of the motif of Abel's sacrifice. A devil below Abel holds a shield-like object that lends its color to the edges of the vest. The flowery vine is a colorful motif that was difficult to capture and translate to multicolor knitting. In this case, I allowed myself artistic freedom as when one embroiders. Despite these limitations the end result was still a very special and colorful garment.

Vest

SIZE: M

FINISHED MEASUREMENTS:

Chest approx. 40 ¼ in / 102 cm

Length: approx. 21 in / 53 cm

YARN: Kampes 2-ply (100% wool; 328 yd / 300 m, 100 g) Sport or equivalent.

YARN AMOUNTS:

Golden yellow 268 approx. 50 g

Orange heather 232 approx. 20 g

White (natural white) approx. 120 g

Malachite green 257 approx. 50 g

Dark turquoise 250 approx. 50 g

Light turquoise heather 251 approx. 40 g

Red-brown 204 approx. 30 g

Medium brown 264 approx. 30 g

NEEDLES: U.S. sizes 1-2 and 2-3 / 2.5 and 3 mm: 16 and 32 in / 40 and 80 cm circulars; U.S. 0 / 2 mm: 16 in / 40 cm circular.

NOTIONS: 10 small buttons, approx. ½ in / 13 mm diameter.

GAUGE: 28 sts and 32 rows in pattern following chart A on largest needles = 4 x 4 in / 10 x 10 cm. Adjust needle sizes to obtain gauge if necessary.

KNITTING TIPS: Begin by reading completely through the instructions. Knit a gauge swatch to make sure you are working at the correct gauge. Note: In order for the motif to show very clearly against the background, it is important that you always bring the pattern color yarn over the background color when changing colors. This method is different than that used for other patterns in this book.
Note: Due to the size of the motif, this vest is designed for one size only.

A
center stitch
▼

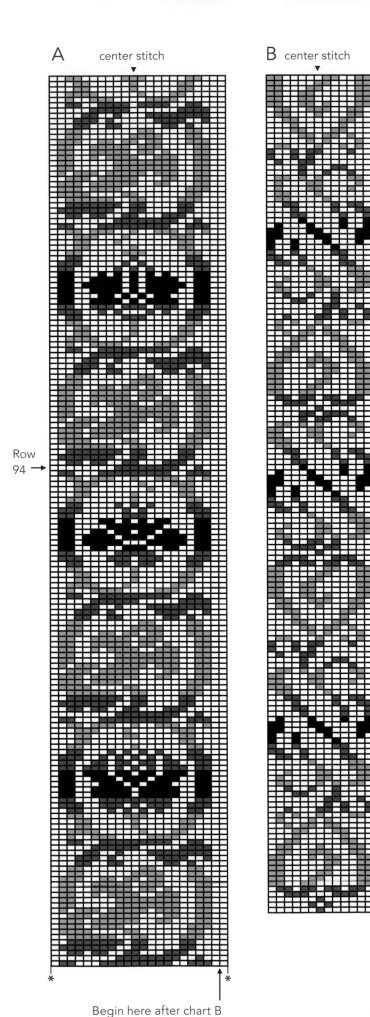

Row
94 →

*   *
Begin here after chart B

B center stitch
▼

BODY: With golden yellow and circular U.S. 1-2 / 2.5 mm, CO 277 sts. Work back and forth in stockinette for 8 rows. Change to orange heather, CO 4 sts, and complete row, ending by casting on CO 4 sts = 285 sts total. Now join to work in the round, making sure that stitches are not twisted. Place marker at beginning of rnd. Knit 1 rnd with orange heather. Change to golden yellow and knit 7 rnds. Cut yarn. Change to circular U.S. 2-3 / 3 mm and work pattern following chart as follows: work 4 steek sts, work 132 sts following chart A, 13 sts following chart B, 132 sts following chart A (begin at arrow on chart), and end with 4 steek sts. The 8 steek sts are for the center front opening and are worked as follows: the outermost st at each side is an edge st and is always knit with MC; the 6 sts in the center of the steek are alternately knit with MC and CC (checkerboard). Don't forget that you should always bring the pattern color (CC) over MC (background) color when changing colors.

Work in pattern for 94 rnds (see arrow on chart A). Next rnd: work 60 sts, place the next 21 sts on a holder, CO 8 sts, work 124 sts, place the following 21 sts on a holder, CO 8 sts, complete rnd. The new sts form the armhole steeks which are worked as for the center front steek. On the next rnd, begin shaping armholes by decreasing outside each steek: ssk to right of steek and k2tog to left of steek. Decrease the same way on every other rnd 11 times. Next, work 10 rnds without decreasing, changing to shorter circular when necessary. On the next rnd, BO the first 3 sts of rnd, work until 3 sts remain and BO last 3 sts. Cut yarn. Place the first 23 sts and last 23 sts of rnd (on the sides of the bound-off sts) = 46 sts total on a holder. CO 4 sts, complete rnd and end by casting on 4 sts. The 8 new sts form the front neck steek which is worked as for the other steeks. Work without shaping for 29 rnds. On the next rnd: place the center 49 sts of back onto a holder for back neck. CO 8 sts for back neck steek and work this steek as for the others. Continue in pattern and, on the next rnd, shape back neck by decreasing 1 st on each side of the steek (k2tog to right of steek and ssk on left); decrease the same way on every other rnd 2 times. Work another 5 rnds without shaping.

Cut MC and continue with white and circular U.S. 1-2 / 2.5 mm. Knit 1 rnd, binding off all steek sts as you work around. Place each set of shoulder sts on a separate holder.

FINISHING: Machine-stitch a line straight down through the 4th and 5th sts (the two center sts) of all steeks. With white yarn, sew a vertical line of duplicate sts over the same sts. Carefully cut open at the center between the center sts, and do not cut into the stitch lines.

Neckband: With golden yellow and circular U.S. 1-2 / 2.5 mm, knit 23 sts from the left side of the center front holder, pick up and knit 32 sts along left side of neck, pick up and knit 8 sts along side of back neck, work 49 sts from the back holder, pick up and knit 8 sts along other side of back neck, pick up and knit 32 sts along right side of front neck, knit 23 sts remaining on front holder = 175 sts total. Work back and forth in stockinette for 5 rows, decreasing at the corners of the front neck with a centered double decrease on every other row (on RS rows) as follows: work to 1 st before the corner st, slip the next st and the corner st knitwise (without knitting them), knit the next st, pass the 2 slipped sts over the last knitted st. Next row: change to orange heather and work 2 rows, continuing to decrease as before. Change to golden yellow and work 6 rows but now, instead of decreasing, increase with M1 on each side of each corner st. BO loosely.

Work the right front band the same way but begin picking up sts at the lower edge. Work 3 rows in stockinette with golden yellow. On the next row (RS): K5, BO 2, *k10, BO 2; rep from * 9 times, k4. On the next row (WS): P4, CO 2, *p10, CO 2; rep from * 9 times and end with p5. Work 2 more rows, change to orange heather, and work 2 rows. Change back to golden yellow and work 4 rows. On the next (RS) row: K5, BO 2, *k10, BO 2; rep from * 9 times, k4. Next row (WS): P4, CO 2, *p10, CO 2; rep from * 9 times and end with p5. Work another 2 rows and then BO loosely on next row.

Armhole bands: With white and short circular U.S. 0 / 2 mm, knit the last 11 sts from the armhole stitch holder, pick up and knit 114 sts evenly spaced around the armhole and knit the remaining 10 sts from holder. Purl 1 rnd, knit 1 rnd, purl 1 rnd. BO knitwise, a bit tightly.

Sew down the steeks on WS with small loose stitches. Fold under the edges and sew to inside with small loose stitches. Weave in all ends. Reinforce buttonhole openings by sewing small stitches over the edge around each hole. Use sewing thread or a finer yarn in a color matching knitting yarn. Lightly steam press the vest under a damp pressing cloth. Sew on buttons.

Härkeberga
Small Leaf Sweater

The little leaf motif that is repeated over the entire Härkeberga Little Leaf sweater is an example of how a seemingly unimportant detail in a painting can inspire an entire garment. In his painted scenes, Albertus Pictor sometimes placed a little tree or bush in the background with elegant ash tree-like leaves, contrasting light against dark or vice versa. On the vault of Härkeberga church, there is such a tree in the scene that shows Esther before King Ahasverus. Another tree is seen in the partially damaged wall paintings to the left of the chancel. I decided to add a dark gold tone to the sweater's yoke.

Sweater

SIZE: S/M (L)

FINISHED MEASUREMENTS:
Chest approx. 41 (46) in / 104 (117) cm
Length: approx. 26 (27 ¼) in / 66 (69) cm
Sleeve length: approx. 19 ¾ (20) in / 50 (51) cm

YARN: Kampes 2-ply (100% wool; 328 yd / 300 m, 100 g) Sport or equivalent.

YARN AMOUNTS:
Black approx. 80 (100) g
Dark turquoise 250 approx. 260 (310) g
Light turquoise 244 approx. 210 (240) g
Old gold 266 approx. 40 (60) g

NEEDLES: U.S. sizes 1-2 and 2-3 / 2.5 and 3 mm: 16 and 32 in / 40 and 80 cm circulars + set of 4 or 5 dpn; U.S. size 8 / 5 mm: 16 in / 40 cm circular; + 1 extra 16 in / 40 cm circular U.S. size 0 or 1-2 / 2 or 2.5 mm to help with picot edgings.

GAUGE: 28 sts and 32 rows in charted pattern on U.S. 2-3 / 3 mm needles = 4 x 4 in / 10 x 10 cm. Adjust needle sizes to obtain gauge if necessary.

KNITTING TIPS: Begin by reading completely through the instructions. Knit a gauge swatch to make sure you are working at the correct gauge. The pattern is repeated over the body in three different colorways:
1: MC – dark turquoise, CC – black.
2: MC – light turquoise, CC – dark turquoise.
3: MC – light turquoise, CC – old gold.
The motif is repeated on the sleeve only in the first 2 colorways. *Note:* The picot edges at the shoulders and top of sleeves can be a little tricky to get right so you may need an extra needle. If you want you can just skip this and work the shoulders the same way on the front and back and continue directly to the rows for the sleeve facing.

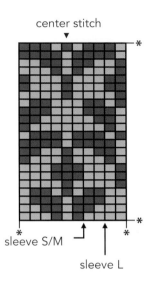

■ MC (main color)
■ CC (contrast/pattern color)

center stitch
▼

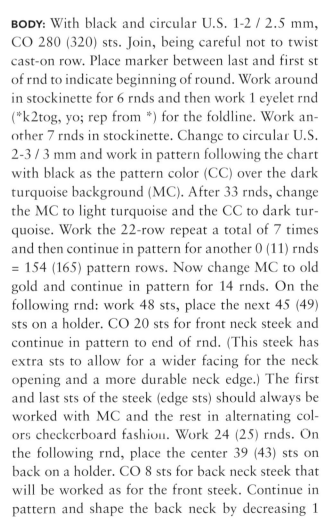

*
sleeve S/M
sleeve L

BODY: With black and circular U.S. 1-2 / 2.5 mm, CO 280 (320) sts. Join, being careful not to twist cast-on row. Place marker between last and first st of rnd to indicate beginning of round. Work around in stockinette for 6 rnds and then work 1 eyelet rnd (*k2tog, yo; rep from *) for the foldline. Work another 7 rnds in stockinette. Change to circular U.S. 2-3 / 3 mm and work in pattern following the chart with black as the pattern color (CC) over the dark turquoise background (MC). After 33 rnds, change the MC to light turquoise and the CC to dark turquoise. Work the 22-row repeat a total of 7 times and then continue in pattern for another 0 (11) rnds = 154 (165) pattern rows. Now change MC to old gold and continue in pattern for 14 rnds. On the following rnd: work 48 sts, place the next 45 (49) sts on a holder. CO 20 sts for front neck steek and continue in pattern to end of rnd. (This steek has extra sts to allow for a wider facing for the neck opening and a more durable neck edge.) The first and last sts of the steek (edge sts) should always be worked with MC and the rest in alternating colors checkerboard fashion. Work 24 (25) rnds. On the following rnd, place the center 39 (43) sts on back on a holder. CO 8 sts for back neck steek that will be worked as for the front steek. Continue in pattern and shape the back neck by decreasing 1

st at each side of the steek (with k2tog to right of steek and ssk to left of steek) on every other round 3 times. Work 2 rounds without shaping. Change to dark turquoise and circular U.S. 1-2 / 2.5 mm: BO 1 st (side st), work 47 (55) sts, BO 20 sts (front neck steek), work 47 (55) sts, BO 1 st (side st), work 47 (55) sts, BO 8 sts (back neck steek), work 47 (55) sts. Place each set of shoulder sts on a separate holder. Place the sts from the left front shoulder on a U.S. 1-2 / 2.5 mm needle. Turn and, on WS, use needles U.S. 8 / 5 mm to purl 1 row. Change back to U.S. 1-2 / 2.5 mm needle and knit 1 row, purl 1 row. On the next (RS) row, work an eyelet row (k2tog, yo) and end the row with k1. Purl 1 row, knit 1 row. Cut yarn. With extra needle, pick up stitches from the loosely knit row on WS, fold at the eyelet row so that the needles are parallel and then join with three-needle bind-off on RS. Work the stitches of the right front shoulder the same way. Place sts on a holder.

SLEEVES: With black and dpn U.S. 1-2 / 2.5 mm, CO 64 (68) sts. Join, being careful not to twist cast-on row. Work in stockinette for 5 rnds and then work an eyelet row as the foldline. Continue in stockinette for 6 more rnds. Change to dpn U.S. 2-3 / 3 mm and work in pattern as for the body, but, only in the first 2 colorways. Begin after the first st of the rnd as indicated with an arrow on the chart—always work the first st of the rnd with MC. On every 4th rnd, increase 2 sts centered at underarm: M1 after the first st of rnd and M1 after the last st. Work the new stitches into the pattern following the chart. Change to circular when stitches fit around. End when the sleeve is approx. 19 ½ (19 ¾) in / 49.5 (50.5) cm long. Cut MC and change to U.S. 1-2 / 2.5 mm and knit 2 rnds with dark turquoise. Change to U.S. 8 / 5 mm and knit 1 row. Change back to U.S. 1-2 / 2.5 mm circular and knit 2 rnds, work an eyelet rnd (k2tog, yo) and then 2 knit rnds. From WS and with extra needle, pick up the stitches from the loosely knitted row. Hold the two needles parallel with RS facing and join with three-needle bind-off. Purl 4 rows for the sleeve facing and, at the same time, increase 2 sts on every row (M1 after and M1 before the first st of row). BO loosely purlwise.

FINISHING: Machine-stitch a line straight down through the two center sts of the front neck steek. Sew a vertical duplicate st row through the same sts and then carefully cut up the center between the stitch lines. Machine-stitch straight down through the 3rd and 6th stitches of back neck steek and cut up the center between the center stitches. Lay one sleeve flat on a flat surface and measure the width at top of sleeve immediately below the facing. Mark the corresponding armhole depth at the sides of the body by basting, with contrast color thread, through the side st, beginning at center of bound-off side st. Machine-stitch 2 lines from the top down on each side of the basting and reinforce with a couple of extra stitches over the side st at the base of the armhole to prevent stitches running. Cut each armhole open through the center of the side stitch, down between the machine-stitched lines. Be careful not to cut into the stitch lines. With the WS facing and dark turquoise yarn, join the shoulders with three-needle bind-off or, with RS facing, Kitchener stitch. For the neck opening use dark turquoise yarn and short circular U.S. 1-2 / 2.5 mm. Pick up 9 sts along right side of back neck, knit 39 (43) sts from back holder, pick up

and knit 9 sts along other side of back neck, knit 29 (30) sts along left side of front neck, knit 45 (49) sts from front holder, pick up and knit 29 (30) sts along right side = 160 (170) sts total. Knit around for 5 rnds, and, at the same time, decrease on every other rnd at the front neck corners as follows: mark the center st of each corner, knit until 1 st before center st, slip the next 2 sts knitwise, k1, p2sso – centered double decrease. Work an eyelet rnd for foldline. Knit another 5 rnds, at the same time, increasing 1 st on each side of each corner st at front on every other rnd. BO loosely.

Sew the front neck steek sts to WS with small loose stitches. Trim the back neck steek to 3-st width and sew to WS with a loose cross stitch row down the length. Fold the facings and neck edging under and sew down securely with loose small stitches to the WS of body. Attach sleeves, fold down facings over the cut edges and sew on inside with small loose stitches. Weave in all ends. Lightly steam press sweater under a damp pressing cloth.

Bromma
Starry Sky Sweater

The stars on the Starry Sky sweater are taken from the wall paintings in Bromma church. The stars in the stenciled paintings were used as space-filling decoration above the sky in various Biblical scenes, as, for example, in the drawing of Mary going to the temple. For the sweater, I used the same colors, with light motifs against the dark background; the stars as the same color as Mary's long and beautiful golden red hair.

Sweater

SIZE: S/M (M/L)

FINISHED MEASUREMENTS:

Chest approx. 40 ½ (42 ½) in / 103 (108) cm

Length: approx. 22 ¾ (23 ½) in / 58 (59.5) cm

Sleeve length: approx. 14 ½ (15 ½) in / 37 (39) cm

YARN: Kampes 2-ply (100% wool; 328 yd / 300 m, 100 g) Sport or equivalent.

YARN AMOUNTS:

Light orange 267 approx. 220 (240) g

Dark orange heather 228 approx. 250 (280) g

NEEDLES: U.S. sizes 1-2 and 2-3 / 2.5 and 3 mm: 16 and 32 in / 40 and 80 cm circulars + set of 4 or 5 dpn.

NOTIONS: Pewter clasp approx. 2 ¼ in / 5.5 cm long (when closed) for top of placket.

GAUGE: 28 sts and 36 rows in pattern following chart A on larger needles = 4 x 4 in / 10 x 10 cm. Adjust needle sizes to obtain gauge if necessary.

KNITTING TIPS: Begin by reading completely through the instructions. Knit a gauge swatch to make sure you are working at the correct gauge. The stitches for the sleeves are picked up around the armholes and the sleeves are worked from the top down. *Note:* This sweater can be knit without the shaped waistline. In that case, CO 348 (360) sts and work ribbing as in the instructions. Decrease 2 (0) sts evenly spaced over the first pattern rnd. Work in pattern following the chart straight up to the armhole, omitting the decreases and increases if you want inset sleeves as in the instructions or work straight up to the shoulder if you'd prefer to re-inforce and cut the armhole open and work drop shoulder sleeves. Don't forget to adjust the sleeve length if you made the drop shoulder sleeves.

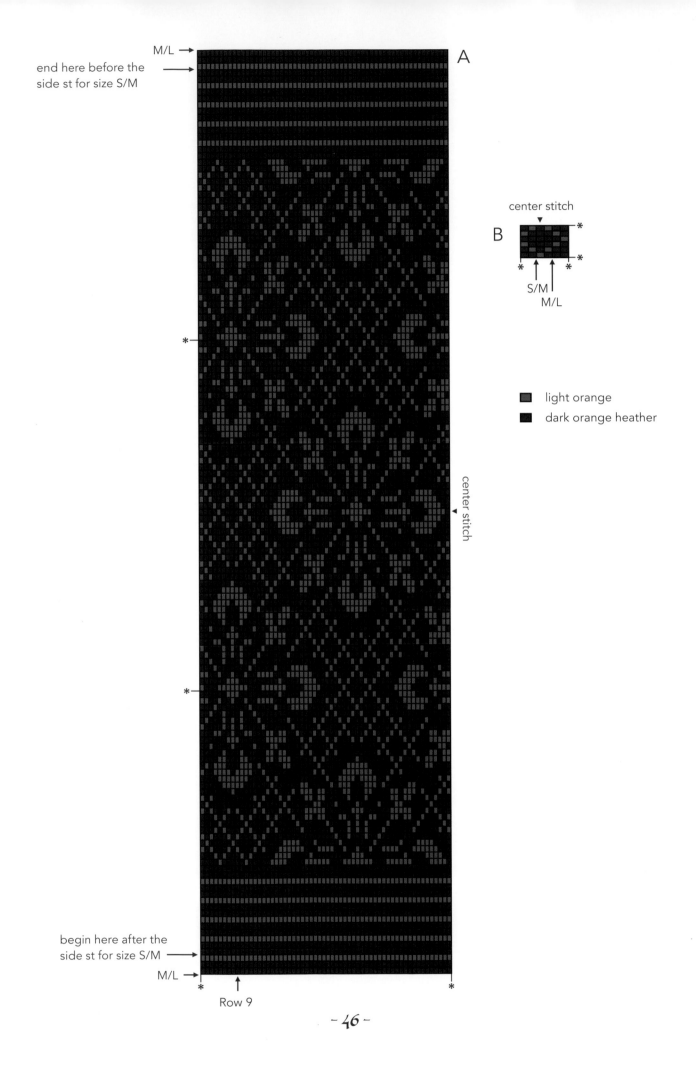

M/L →

end here before the
side st for size S/M

A

center stitch
▼

B

*

*

*

S/M

M/L

■ light orange
■ dark orange heather

*

center stitch ◄

*

begin here after the
side st for size S/M →

M/L →

*

Row 9 ↑

*

BODY: With light orange and smaller circular, CO 324 (336) sts; join, being careful not to twist cast-on row. Place marker between the last and first st to indicate beginning of round. Work ribbing in the round as follows:

Rnd 1: P3, *k2, sl 1, k2tog, psso, k2, p5; rep from * around and end with p2.

Rnds 2-5: P3, *K5, p5; rep from * around and end with p2 = 270 (280) sts remain.

Change to larger circular and begin at arrow for your size, following pattern on chart A. Note: Size S/M begins on chart row 9. The chart is worked 2 times per round; the first st of the rnd and the st before the chart repeat is a side st that should always be knit with light orange. (The chart does not show the side st or the shaping with decreases and increases at the sides). The front and back are worked the same way up to the front placket.

Note: At the same time as the chart's first row is worked, increase 6 (8) sts evenly spaced over the front and back. These sts are worked in pattern following the chart. Place a second marker after 138 (144) sts (before the second side st of the rnd) to indicate where the back begins. The rnd now has a total of 276 (288) sts.

Continue without increasing and work in pattern for a total of 12 (15) rnds. On the next rnd, decrease 1 st on each side of the side sts with k2tog left of the side st and ssk on right side of side st. Decrease the same way on every 4th (6th) rnd another 6 (5) times = 248 (264) sts.

Continue without shaping for 11 (7) rnds. On the next rnd, increase 1 st with M1 on each side of each side st and then on every 5th (6th) rnd 9 (8) times = 288 (300) sts; work new sts into pattern. Now work without shaping for another 14 (12) rnds. On the next rnd: cut yarn and place the first 9 sts of the rnd on a holder; CO 4 sts, work 127 (133) sts, place the next 17 sts on a holder, CO 8 sts and work 127 (133) sts, place the last 8 sts of rnd on a holder (same holder that has the first 9 sts), and CO 4 sts. The newly cast-on sts form the armhole steeks. The first and last sts of each steek are edge sts that should always be knit with dark orange heather; work the remaining steek sts alternating colors checkerboard fashion. Continue

working in the round without shaping for 28 (30) rnds. Next rnd: work 64 (67) sts, place the next 7 sts on a holder for neck placket, CO 8 sts for the placket steek (work as for armhole steeks), and complete rnd in pattern. Work in pattern for another 24 rnds. Next rnd: Work 63 (67) sts, cut dark orange heather and BO 8 sts (steek); reattach dark orange and continue with both yarns and complete rnd in pattern.

On the following rnd, work 51 (54) sts, place the next 26 sts on a holder (13 sts from each side of the placket steek's bound-off sts), CO 8 sts for a front neck steek (working steek as before) and complete round in pattern. Begin shaping the front neck, decreasing 1 st (k2tog to right of neck and ssk on left) on each side of the front neck on the next rnd and then on every rnd 5 times; next, decrease on every other rnd 3 times. Work without further shaping for 5 rnds. On the next rnd, place the center 45 sts of back on a holder for back neck. CO 8 sts for a back neck steek (work as for other steeks). Continue working in pattern and decrease for the back neck on the next rnd with 1 st on each side of the steek's edge sts and then on every other rnd 2 times. Work 1 rnd without decreases. Cut dark orange heather, change to smaller circular and knit 1 rnd with light orange. Next row: BO 4 sts (steek), work 38 (41) sts, BO the front neck steek sts, work 38 (41) sts, BO 8 sts, work 38 (41) sts, BO back neck steek, work 38 (41) sts, BO 4 sts. Place each set of shoulder sts on a separate holder.

SLEEVES: Using back stitch, hand-sew a line working from the top down through the 2nd and 7th sts in every steek and then cut up the center of each steek between the center sts. Join shoulders with three-needle bind-off or Kitchener stitch using light orange yarn. Begin with right sleeve and, with dark orange heather and short, larger size circular, pick up and knit 131 (135) sts in edge sts of armhole steek, beginning at the underarm and towards the back of the sweater. Work back and forth in pattern following chart B for 9 rows (see arrow for your size). Next row: CO 1 st and continue in pattern but now work in the round; the first st of the rnd is always knit with dark orange heather. On the 4th rnd, decrease 1 st on each side of the first st of the rnd (on the left side with k2tog and with ssk on the right side); decrease a total of 26 (28) times = 80 sts remain. Change to dpn when sts no longer fit around circular. Continue without further shaping for 2 (1) rnds. Change to smaller dpn and knit 1 rnd with dark orange heather. Change to light orange and knit 1 rnd and then work in rib for 4 rnds as follows: P3, *k5, p5; rep from * around, ending with p2. On the next rnd, work p3, *k2, knit 3 sts into the next st: work 1 st through the back loop, 1 st into front loop and the last st by lifting the vertical strand between the previous 2 sts and knitting into it, k2, p5; rep from * around, ending with p2. BO purlwise. Make the left sleeve the same way but begin at underarm and pick up sts towards the front of the sweater. Seam the underarm with RS facing and Kitchener stitch.

FINISHING: The neckband is worked with the smaller circular and light orange. Work 13 sts from front holder to the left of the placket, pick up and knit 20 sts along left side of neck, pick up and knit 7 sts along right side of back neck, knit 45 sts from back holder, pick up and knit 7 sts along left back neck, pick up and knit 20 sts along right side of neck and then knit remaining 13 sts from front holder = 125 sts total. Turn and begin ribbing back and forth (the first row is worked on WS) with *P5, k5; rep from * and end with p5 [on the RS repeat (k5, p5) and end with k5.]

Neck Placket: With light orange and smaller circular, pick up and knit 25 sts in the edge sts to the left of the front placket, beginning at the base of the placket and ending with sts over the neck band. Work 3 rows (the 1st row = WS) back and forth in ribbing as follows: *P5, k5; rep from * and end with p5. Place the sts on a holder. Work the right placket edge to correspond, but begin at the top at the neck by picking up sts at top of neckband. BO on RS purlwise, knit 1 st in the center of the saved 7 placket sts and then BO the center st; continue and knit and BO with an extra needle. Join the lower edges of the placket to the rest of the saved sts at the bottom of the placket with Kitchener stitch. Trim all the steeks to 3-st width (including edge sts) and sew down on inside with a loose cross stitches down the length. Weave in all ends. Lightly steam press the sweater under a damp pressing cloth. Sew the clasp to top edge of placket.

The Mälar Valley School

The Mälar Valley School covers several different styles, and, although generally considered as rather deficient in figure painting, is characterized by its graceful vines, such as these grapevines on the vault in Villberga church. The garments in this section were inspired primarily by the paintings in Norrsunda church, but Villberga and Litslena are also represented with their own designs.

Norrsunda
Angel with Pillar Cardigan

The motif that decorates the Angel with Pillars cardigan is a type of plump trefoil with a simple leaf vein. It is taken from a painted angel in Norrsunda church who, is holding something that looks like a pillar in one hand and is dressed in a floor-length garment decorated with this three leaf pattern. I took inspiration for the bottom panels from the swirling flower vines around the angel, framing them with colors from the wings.

Cardigan

SIZE: S (M/L)

FINISHED MEASUREMENTS:
Chest approx. 38 ¼ (44) in / 97 (112) cm
Length: approx. 21 ¼ (22 ½) in / 54 (57) cm
Sleeve length: approx. 19 (19 ¾) in / 48 (50) cm

YARN: Kampes 2-ply (100% wool; 328 yd / 300 m, 100 g) Sport or equivalent.

YARN AMOUNTS:
White (natural white approx. 240 (280) g
Orange heather 232 approx. 150 (170) g
Dark blue 224 approx. 100 (110) g
Dark blue-gray 242 approx. 20 (20) g
Medium brown 264 approx. 10 (10) g
Light turquoise 244 approx. 10 (10) g
Small amounts red-brown 204 and light green 258

NEEDLES: U.S. sizes 2-3 and 4 / 3 and 3.5 mm: 16 and 32 in / 40 and 80 cm circulars + set of 4 or 5 dpn.

NOTIONS: 8 half-round ball buttons approx. ½ in / 13 mm diameter

GAUGE: 26 sts and 29 rows in pattern following chart B on larger needles = 4 x 4 in / 10 x 10 cm. Adjust needle sizes to obtain gauge if necessary.

KNITTING TIPS: Begin by reading completely through the instructions. Knit a gauge swatch to make sure you are working at the correct gauge. All the single-color sections are worked with smaller size needles and the two-color sections with the larger needles. *Note:* The panels on the lower edges have flowers and leaves that are emphasized with duplicate stitch in various colors. If you want a more subdued look for your garment, omit the embroidery on the panels.

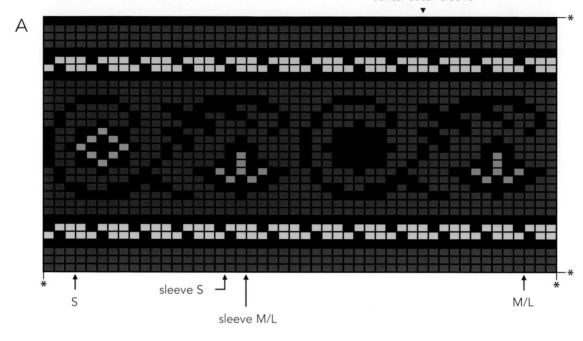

center stitch sleeve

A

*

sleeve S

sleeve M/L

S

M/L

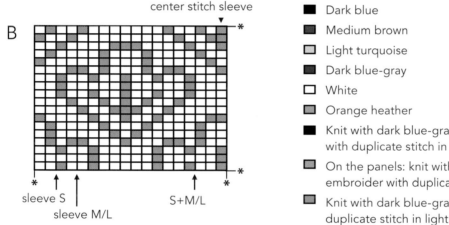

center stitch sleeve

B

sleeve S

sleeve M/L

S+M/L

- ■ Dark blue
- ■ Medium brown
- □ Light turquoise
- ■ Dark blue-gray
- □ White
- ■ Orange heather
- ■ Knit with dark blue-gray and embroider with duplicate stitch in red-brown
- ■ On the panels: knit with dark blue-gray and embroider with duplicate stitch in orange heather
- ■ Knit with dark blue-gray and embroider with duplicate stitch in light green

BODY: With dark blue and smaller size circular, CO 252 (288) sts; join, being careful not to twist cast-on row. Place a marker between the last and first sts of the rnd to indicate beginning of rnd. The first and last 2 sts of the round are steek sts for the center front. On pattern rows, always knit the first and last of the steek's 4 sts with MC (edge sts) and alternate colors on the other 2 sts checkerboard fashion. Work 6 rnds in stockinette and then work an eyelet rnd for the foldline as follows: 2 steek sts, *k2tog, yo; rep from * until 4 sts remain and end with k2tog, 2 steek sts – 251 (287) sts. Work in stockinette for another 7 rnds. Now work in pattern following chart A, beginning at arrow for your size.

Don't forget to work the single-color rnds with the smaller needle and the two-color rnds with

larger needles. After completing the 32 rows of chart A, continue with chart B, beginning at the arrow for your size. Repeat pattern on chart B until piece measures almost 21 ¼ (22 ½) in / 54 (57) cm long or until a total of 158 (167) rnds have been worked. On the next rnd, BO the first 2 and last 2 sts (steek sts). Cut yarn and place remaining sts on a holder.

SLEEVES: With dark blue and smaller dpn, CO 60 (64) sts; join, being careful not to twist cast-on row. Work around in stockinette for 6 rnds and then work the eyelet rnd (k2tog, yo) around for foldline. Work another 7 rnds in stockinette. Now work the pattern on chart A, beginning after the first st of the rnd at the arrow for the sleeves; the first st of

every round should always be knit with MC. On every 4th rnd, increase with M1 after the first st and M1 after the last st of the round. Work new sts into charted pattern. Don't forget to work the single-color rnds with the smaller needle and the two-color rnds with larger needles. After completing chart A, continue with pattern on chart B, increasing on every 4th rnd (change to circular when sts fit around). When sleeve is 19 (19 ¾) in / 48 (50) cm long, cut CC and, with MC and smaller needle, knit 1 rnd. Now purl 4 rnds for facing, increasing after first and after last st on every purl rnd. BO loosely.

FINISHING: Lay one of the sleeves flat on a flat surface and measure the width at the top of the sleeve just below the facing and mark the corresponding armhole depth on the body by hand-stitching, with contrast color thread, straight down beginning at the center of the side st. Machine-stitch 2 lines from the top down on each side of the basting and reinforce with a couple of extra sts over the side st at the base of the armhole to avoid stitches running. Cut the armhole open through the center of each side st and down between the machine-stitched lines, being careful not to cut through the stitched lines. Machine-stitch two parallel lines from the top down in each of the center sts on the front steek. Cut open between these lines at center of steek. Join shoulders with three-needle bind-off or Kitchener stitch, leaving approx. 6 ¾ (7) in / 17 (18) cm in the center open for the neck. Mark the neck shaping, hand basting the cutting lines with a contrast color thread, forming an arc approx. 4 in / 10 cm deep at center front and 3/8 in / 1 cm deep on the back. Machine-stitch parallel lines just outside the basting and then cut away excess fabric.

Front and neck bands: With dark blue and smaller needles, CO 14 sts and work back and forth in stockinette until piece measures approx. 59 (62 ¼) in / 150 (158) cm. Do not cut yarn; place sts on a holder in case you need to shorten or lengthen the band. Baste the band with RS facing RS around the front edges and neck of the sweater; adjust and BO. Sew the band on securely by machine or with back stitch by hand. Fold the band and lightly press it and then fold the band over the cut edges of the steek and sew down by hand to WS with small loose stitches. Attach sleeves; fold facing over the cut edges and sew down on WS with small loose stitches. Weave in all ends. Lightly steam press the sweater under a damp pressing cloth. Sew or crochet 8 small button loops with dark blue yarn along the edge of the right front and then sew the buttons on the left front.

Norrsunda
Wreath Pullover

The motif for this sweater comes from the Norrsunda church. The open wreath is featured in several scenes in the church's paintings and this one appears, in various color combinations, in a brocade-like pattern on clothing. I tried to capture the same brown and rust-colored tones as they are today on Pilate's garment, but added an edging in malachite green for some contrast.

Pullover

SIZE: Men's S (M, L)

FINISHED MEASUREMENTS:
Chest approx. 43 ¼ (47 ¼, 51 ¼) in / 110 (120, 130) cm
Length: approx. 26 (27 ¼, 28 ¾) in / 66.5 (69, 73) cm
Sleeve length: approx. 20 (20, 20 ½) in / 51 (51, 52) cm

YARN: Kampes 2-ply (100% wool; 328 yd / 300 m, 100 g) Sport or equivalent.

YARN AMOUNTS:
Malachite green 257 approx. 20 (20, 20) g
Dark red-brown 253 approx. 260 (310, 310) g
Red-brown 204 approx. 180 (180, 210) g
Medium brown 264 approx. 160 (180, 180) g
Dark orange heather 228 approx. 80 (90, 90) g

NEEDLES: U.S. sizes 2-3 and 4 / 3 and 3.5 mm: 16 and 32 in / 40 and 80 cm circulars + set of 4 or 5 dpn.

GAUGE: 26 sts and 28 rows in pattern following chart A on larger needles = 4 x 4 in / 10 x 10 cm. Adjust needle sizes to obtain gauge if necessary.

KNITTING TIPS: Begin by reading completely through the instructions. Knit a gauge swatch to make sure you are working at the correct gauge.
Note: There are some small differences between charts A and B so that motif will fit the various sizes. The wreaths are spaced a little more closely together in size M than for sizes S and L.

■ dark red-brown
■ red-brown
■ medium brown
■ dark orange heather

center stitch
▼

A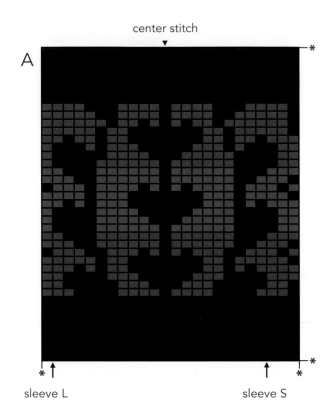
*

*   *
↑   ↑   *
sleeve L   sleeve S

center stitch
▼

B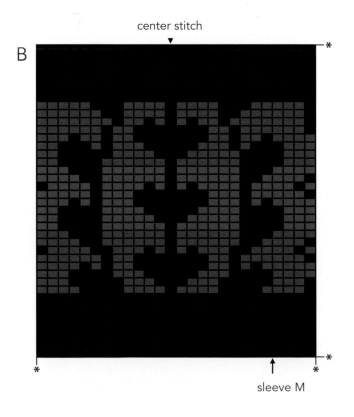
*

*

*
↑   *
sleeve M

BODY: With malachite green and smaller circular, CO 272 (294, 316) sts; join, being careful not to twist cast-on row and place marker between last and first st of rnd to indicate beginning of rnd. Work 2 rnds k2, p2 rib. Now work 2-color rib with dark red-brown for all the knit sts. For the purl stitches, alternate 2 rnds each red-brown, medium brown, and dark orange heather. Repeat these 6 rnds 2 more times = 18 rnds total. Knit 1 rnd with red-brown and, at the same time, increase 16 (18, 20) sts evenly spaced around = 288 (312, 336) sts total. Change to larger circular and work in pattern following chart A (B, A) until piece measures approx. 23 ½ (24 ½, 26) in / 59.5 (62, 66) cm or until 145 (152, 160) pattern rows have been worked.

Next rnd: Work 57 (62, 68) sts, place 31 (33, 33) sts on a holder for the front neck. CO 10 sts for front neck steek. The first and last sts of the steek are edge sts and should always be knit with MC; work remaining steek sts alternating colors checkerboard fashion. Continue working around, decreasing 1 st on each side of the neck (k2tog on right side of neck and ssk on left) on every rnd 5 times and then on every other rnd 3 times. Work 1 more rnd without decreasing.

Next rnd: Place the center 41 (43, 43) sts of back on a holder and then CO 10 sts for back neck steek (work as for front neck steek). On next rnd, decrease 1 st on each side of neck steek and then decrease on every other rnd 2 times; work 0 (1, 1) rnds without decreasing. Change to smaller circular and dark red-brown and knit 2 rnds. Next rnd: BO 1 st, work 48 (53, 59) sts, BO 10 sts of front neck steek, work 48 (53, 59) sts, BO 1 st, work 48 (53, 59) sts, BO 10 sts of back neck steek, and complete rnd. Place each set of shoulder sts on a separate holder.

SLEEVES: With malachite green and smaller dpn, CO 56 (60, 64) sts; join and work 2 rnds in k2, p2 rib. Cut yarn and work in 2-color rib as for bottom edge of body. Change to red-brown and knit 1 rnd, increasing 12 sts evenly spaced around to 68 (72, 76) sts total. Change to larger dpn and work in pattern following chart A (B, A). Begin after the first st on the rnd at the arrow for your size; the first st of the round is always knit with MC. On every 4th rnd, increase with M1 on each side of the first st (center of underarm). Work new sts into charted pattern and change to larger size circular when sts fit around. Continue as set until sleeve is approx. 19 ¾ (19 ¾, 20 ¼) in / 50.5 (50.5, 51.5) cm long. Change to smaller circular and dark red-brown and knit 2 rnds without increasing. With dark red-brown purl 4 rnds for a facing, increasing with M1 on each side of the first st of rnd on every purl rnd. BO loosely.

FINISHING: Hand-stitch a line of back stitches through the 2nd and 9th sts of each neck steek and then cut steek open through the center of the center stitch. Lay a sleeve flat on a flat surface and measure the width at the sleeve top just below the reverse stockinette facing. Mark the corresponding width for the armhole depth on the body by basting, with a contrast color thread, straight down from the center of the bound-off side st. Machine-stitch 2 lines on each side of the basting and reinforce with an extra couple of stitches over the side st at the base of the armhole to avoid stitches running. Cut open in the center between the stitch lines. Avoid cutting into the stitch lines because the stitches might unravel. Join shoulders with three-needle bind-off or Kitchener stitch.

Neckband: With RS facing, red-brown, and short smaller size circular, pick up and knit 6 (8, 8) sts along right side of back neck, knit the sts from back stitch holder, pick up and knit 6 (8, 8) sts along left side, 18 (20, 20) sts along left side of front neck, knit stitches from the front holder, pick up and knit 18 (20, 20) sts along right front neck side = 120 (132, 132) sts total. Work around in k2, p2 rib as for lower edge with knit sts in dark red-brown and purl sts alternating dark orange heather, medium brown and red-brown for 2 rnds each. Finish with 2 rnds rib with malachite green. BO loosely in ribbing. Trim the steeks to 3-stitch width and secure to WS with a loose cross stitch row down the length. Attach sleeves, fold facing over cut edges and sew down securely on WS with small loose stitches. Weave in all ends. Lightly steam press sweater (do not press ribbing) under a damp pressing cloth.

Norrsunda
Saint's Flower Vest

argareta is one of the saints pictured in the Norrsunda church. Her dress features a flowery brocade-like pattern which also appears in various color combinations in the church's paintings. The Saint's Flower vest and child's sweater has a yoke with the motif in reversed colors and two-color ribbing at the lower edge; the vest also has two-color ribbing at the neck. The colors for the ribbing are taken from the swirling flowery wreaths that surround the figures in this part of the paintings.

Vest

SIZES: S/M (L)

FINISHED MEASUREMENTS:
Chest approx. 41 (45 ¼) in / 104 (115) cm
Length: approx. 24 ½ (25) in / 62 (63.5) cm
YARN: Kampes 2-ply (100% wool; 328 yd / 300 m, 100 g) Sport or equivalent.

YARN AMOUNTS:
White (natural white) approx. 170 (190) g
Dark blue-gray 242 approx. 140 (160) g
Red-brown 204 approx. 25 (30) g
Orange heather 232 approx. 35 (40 g)
NEEDLES: U.S. size 0 / 2 mm: 16 in / 40 cm circular; U.S. sizes 1-2 and 2-3 / 2.5 and 3 mm: 16 and 32 in / 40 and 80 cm circulars.
GAUGE: 28 sts and 32 rows in pattern following chart A on largest needles = 4 x 4 in / 10 x 10 cm. Adjust needle sizes to obtain gauge if necessary.
KNITTING TIPS: Begin by reading completely through the instructions. Knit a gauge swatch to make sure you are working at the correct gauge.
Note: Because the armhole and neck steeks replace a larger number of stitches, you may need to use a shorter circular if the stitches do not fit around the longer needle.

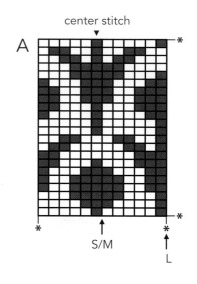

center stitch

A

S/M

L

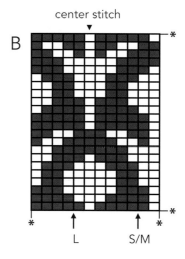

center stitch

B

L   S/M

□ white
■ dark blue-gray

BODY: With red-brown and U.S. 1-2 / 2.5 mm circular, CO 288 (312) sts; join, being careful not to twist cast-on row. Place marker between last and first sts to indicate beginning of rnd. Work in two-color rib for 2 in / 5 cm: work k2, p2 rib with red-brown for the knit sts and orange heather for the purl sts. Cut yarn and change to U.S. 2-3 / 3 mm circular and dark gray-blue and white yarns. Work in pattern following chart A, beginning at the arrow for your size. Work the 22-row pattern repeat a total of 4 times and then continue in pattern for another 19 rnds = 107 pattern rnds. Cut yarn and place the first 13 sts of the rnd on a holder. CO 4 sts and work 119 (131) sts; place the next 25 sts on a holder and CO 8 sts; work 119 (131) sts, and place the last 12 sts on the holder with the first 13 sts, CO 4 sts. The new sts are the armhole steeks. The first and last st of each steek is an edge st and should always be knit with MC; the remaining steek sts alternate colors checkerboard fashion. Continue working in the round following the chart for 1 rnd and then decrease 1 st on each side of the steeks on every other rnd 11 times: work ssk on the left side of the steek and k2tog on the right side.

Note: On the same rnd as the 7th decreases, after 120 rnds of pattern knitting, begin working the pattern following chart B.

When all the decreases have been completed, work 9 (14) rnds without shaping. On the next rnd: work 28 (32) sts, place the center front 49 (53) sts on a holder, CO 8 sts for front neck steek, and complete rnd. Work the front neck steek as for armhole steeks. Continue in pattern for 35 rnds. On the next rnd, make a back neck steek: work through the second armhole steek [27 (31) sts], place the next 43 (47) sts at center back on a holder, CO 8 sts for back neck steek and complete rnd. Work the back neck steek as for front steek but decrease 1 st (k2tog on right side and ssk on left) on every other rnd on each side of the steek a total of 3 times = 181 (190) total pattern rnds. Cut yarn and knit 1 rnd with red-brown yarn and U.S. 1-2 / 2.5 mm circular. On the next rnd, BO all the steek sts. Place the remaining sts on a holder.

FINISHING: Machine-stitch a vertical line down through each of the two center stitches in all the steeks. Sew a vertical line of duplicate stitches with white yarn over these sts. Carefully cut up the center between the stitchlines, avoiding cutting into the stitches. Turn the garment inside out and join shoulders with three-needle bind-off or, with RS out, Kitchener stitch.

Armhole bands: With white and short circular U.S. 0 / 2 mm, knit the last 13 sts from the armhole stitch holders, pick up and knit 124 (132) sts around the armhole and knit the remaining 12 sts from the holder = 149 (157) sts. Work around: purl 1 rnd, knit 1 rnd, purl 1 rnd. BO knitwise a bit tightly.

Neckband: Prepare the neck ribbing by picking up 176 sts with the short circular U.S. 1-2 / 2.5 mm, alternating k2 with red-brown and k2 with orange heather; begin the rnd by picking up 1 st with red-brown, followed by 2 sts with orange heather and then follow the 2-2 sequence. Pick up a total of 7 sts along the right side of the back neck, knit 42 (46) sts from the back holder and, *at the same time,* decrease 1 st at center back, pick up and knit 7 sts along left side of back neck, 36 sts along left side of front neck, knit 48 (52) sts from the front holder and, *at the same time,* decrease 1 st at center front, pick up and knit 36 sts along the right side of front neck. Work in two-color, k2, p2 rib for 4 rnds. Begin and end the rnd with k1 in red-brown. On these 4 rnds, *at the same time* decrease at front neck corners on every other rnd as follows: mark the corner's 2 center sts (which should always be knit with red-brown), work to 1 st before center stitch. With red-brown, knit the next st together with the first corner st. Slip the next corner st, knit the next st with red-brown, psso. After 4 rnds of two-color rib, work 1 rnd rib with U.S. 1-2 / 2.5 mm needle and red-brown. BO in rib rather tightly. Sew down the steeks by hand to WS with small loose stitches. Weave in all ends. Lightly steam press (except for ribbing) the vest under a damp pressing cloth.

Norrsunda
Saint's Flower Child's Sweater

Child's Sweater

SIZES: 4 (6, 8) years

FINISHED MEASUREMENTS:

Chest approx. 29 ¼ (32 ¾, 36 ¼) in / 74 (83, 92) cm

Length: approx. 16 ½ (18 ¼, 19 ¾) in / 42 (46, 50) cm

Sleeve length: approx. 11 ¾ (13 ¾, 15 ½) in / 30 (35, 39) cm

YARN: Kampes 2-ply (100% wool; 328 yd / 300 m, 100 g) Sport or equivalent.

YARN AMOUNTS:

White (natural white) approx. 130 (160, 190) g

Dark blue-gray 242 approx. 120 (150, 170) g

Red-brown 204 approx. 30 (30, 30) g

Orange heather 232 approx. 20 (20, 20 g)

NEEDLES: U.S. sizes 2-3 and 4 / 3 and 3.5 mm: 16 and 24 in / 40 and 60 cm circulars + set of 4 or 5 dpn.

GAUGE: 26 sts and 30 rows in pattern following chart A on larger needles = 4 x 4 in / 10 x 10 cm. Adjust needle sizes to obtain gauge if necessary.

KNITTING TIPS: Begin by reading completely through the instructions. Knit a gauge swatch to make sure you are working at the correct gauge. The body of the sweater is worked around in one piece up to the front neck. After that point, the body is worked back and forth with knit and purl rows.

center stitch

A

center stitch

B

sleeve
4 and 6
years

sleeve
8 years

4 and 8 years

6 years

□ white
■ dark blue-gray

BODY: With red-brown and smaller circular, CO 184 (204, 228) sts; join, being careful not to twist cast-on sts. Place a marker between last and first sts to indicate beginning of rnd. Work in two-color k2, p2 rib for 2 in / 5 cm with red-brown for the knit sts and orange heather for the purl sts. Cut yarn and, with white, knit 1 rnd, increasing 8 (12, 12) sts evenly spaced around = 192 (216, 240) sts total. Change to larger circular and work in pattern following chart A. Work the 22-row repeat a total of 3 (4, 4) times and then work another 12 (0, 12) rnds = 78 (88, 100) rnds in pattern. Change to chart B, beginning at the arrow for your size, and work 10 rnds following the chart; cut yarn.

Front neck: Skip 28 (34, 40) sts, place the next 41 sts on a holder. The row now begins to the left of the front neck. Continue working back and forth in pattern over the remaining sts for 15 rows. On the next row: work 58 (70, 82) sts, place the center 35 sts on a holder and turn. From this point, each side of the neck is worked separately, beginning at the right shoulder. Decrease on each side of the back neck by binding off 1 st on every other row 3 times. Continue in pattern without decreasing until a total of 32 rows have been worked following chart B. Change to red-brown and smaller circular and knit 1 row. On the next row, work 27 (33, 39) sts, BO 1 st (side st), work 27 (33, 39) sts. Place each set of shoulder sts on a separate holder. Work the left shoulder the same way, reversing shaping.

SLEEVES: With red-brown and smaller dpn, CO 48 (48, 52) sts, join and work in two-color rib for 2 in / 5 cm as for body. Cut yarn and attach white. Work 1 rnd, increasing 8 sts evenly spaced around = 56 (56, 60) sts. Change to larger dpn and work in pattern following chart A. Begin at arrow for sleeve, starting after the first st of the round which is always worked with MC. Work new sts into charted pattern. Change to circular when stitches fit around.

Sizes 4 and 6 years: Increase 2 sts centered on underarm (M1 after the first st and M1 after the last st) on every 3rd rnd.

Size 8 years: Increase 2 sts centered on underarm on every 3rd rnd (M1 after the first st and M1 after the last st) 15 times and then on every 4th rnd 13 times = 116 sts. *All sizes:* After all increases have been worked, continue in pattern without further shaping until sleeve is 11 ½ (13 ½, 15 ¼) in / 29.5 (34.5, 38.5) cm long or almost desired length. Cut yarn; change to red-brown and smaller circular; knit 2 rnds. Now purl 4 rnds for the facing, increasing 2 sts centered at underarm: M1 after the first st and M1 after the last st. BO loosely.

FINISHING: Lay one sleeve flat on a flat surface and measure the width of the sleeve top immediately below the reverse stockinette facing. Mark the corresponding armhole depth on the body by hand-stitching, with contrast color thread, straight down starting in the center of the bound-off side stitch. Machine-stitch 2 lines on each side of the basting and reinforce with a couple of extra stitches over the side st at the base of the armhole to prevent the stitches from running. Cut armhole up the center through the center st and down between the machine stitched lines, being careful not to cut through the stitch lines. Join shoulders with Kitchener stitch or, with RS facing RS, with three-needle bind-off, using red-brown yarn.

Neckband: With short smaller size circular and red-brown, pick up and knit 6 sts along the right side of the back neck, knit 35 sts from the back holder, pick up and knit 6 sts along left side of back neck, 18 sts along left side of front neck, knit 41 st from front holder, pick up and knit 18 sts along right side of front neck = 124 sts. Join and work around in k1, p1 rib for 5 rnds and, *at the same time*, decrease at front neck corners on every other rnd as follows: mark the center st of each corner (the 65th and 107th sts of rnd), work to 2 sts before center st (which is always knitted). If the next to last st before the corner's center st is knit, ssk, work center st, k2tog. If the next to last st before center st is purl, p2tog, knit corner center st, p2tog. BO loosely in ribbing. Attach sleeves, folding facing over the cut edges. Sew facing down by hand with small loose stitches to WS. Weave in all ends. Lightly steam press (except for ribbing) under a damp pressing cloth.

Norrsunda Trefoil Sweater

The trefoil motif adapted from the paintings in Norrsunda church is one of the prettiest I've seen. The motif, used to decorate the clothing of various figures, is a brocade-like pattern, shown in least a couple of color combinations. The combination I was drawn to is on Gertrude of Nivelle's lovely floor-length dress. The edges of the sweater owe their colors to the lining of Gertrude's cloak and the ash-colored cloud she is standing on.

Sweater

SIZES: M (L)

FINISHED MEASUREMENTS:

Chest approx. 43 ¼ (48) in / 110 (122) cm
Length: approx. 26 ½ (27 ¼) in / 67 (69.5) cm
Sleeve length: approx. 19 (19 ¼) in / 48 (49) cm

YARN: Kampes 2-ply (100% wool; 328 yd / 300 m, 100 g) Sport or equivalent.

YARN AMOUNTS:

Red-brown 204 approx. 330 (380) g
Pale old rose 269 approx. 240 (280) g
Dark blue-gray 242 approx. 50 (60) g
Malachite green 257 approx. 10 (10) g

NEEDLES: U.S. sizes 2-3 and 4 / 3 and 3.5 mm: 16 and 32 in / 40 and 80 cm circulars + set of 4 or 5 dpn.

GAUGE: 26 sts and 29 rows in charted pattern on larger needles = 4 x 4 in / 10 x 10 cm.
Adjust needle sizes to obtain gauge if necessary.

KNITTING TIPS: Begin by reading completely through the instructions. Knit a gauge swatch to make sure you are working at the correct gauge.

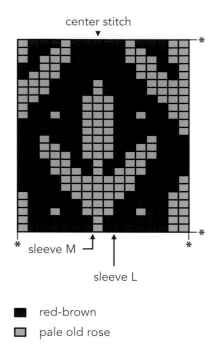

center stitch ▼

* sleeve M ⌐
sleeve L

■ red-brown
▨ pale old rose

BODY: With dark blue-gray and smaller circular, CO 288 (320) sts; join, being careful not to twist cast-on row. Place a marker between last and first st to indicate beginning of rnd. Work 7 rnds in stockinette. Change to malachite green and work an eyelet rnd (*k2tog, yo; rep from * around) as the foldline. Knit 2 more rnds with malachite green and then change to dark blue-gray and knit 6 rnds. Change to larger circular and work in charted pattern until piece measures approx. 21 ¾ (22 ¾) in / 55.5 (58) cm or until 156 (163) pattern rows have been worked.

Next rnd: Work 49 (57) sts, place the next 47 sts on a holder for the front neck. CO 20 sts for a front neck steek and continue working in the round. (The steek has extra sts to allow for a wider facing and more stable neckline). Always knit the first and last sts of the steek with red-brown as edge sts with the remaining sts alternating colors in checkerboard fashion.

Continue straight up for 24 rnds (approx. 3 ¼ in / 8.5 cm). On the next rnd, place the center 43 sts of back on a holder. CO 8 sts for a back neck steek and work it as for front neck steek. Shape back

neck by decreasing on every other rnd 2 times, with k2tog on the right side and ssk on the left side of steek. Change to smaller circular and dark blue-gray and work 1 rnd. Next rnd: BO 1 st (side st), work 48 (56) sts, BO 20 sts (front neck steek), work 48 (56) sts, BO 1 st (side st), work 48 (56) sts, BO 8 sts (back neck steek), work 48 (56) sts. Place each set of shoulder sts on a separate holder.

SLEEVES: With dark blue-gray and smaller dpn, CO 64 (68) sts; join, being careful not to twist cast-on row. Work 6 rnds stockinette. Change to malachite green and work 1 eyelet rnd for foldline. Work 2 more rnds in stockinette with malachite green and then change to dark blue-gray and knit 5 rnds. Change to larger dpn and work in pattern as for body. Begin pattern after the first st of the round at the arrow for the sleeves on the chart; always knit the first st of the round with MC. On every 4th rnd, increase with M1 after the first and M1 after the last st; work new sts into pattern. Change to circular when sts fit around. When sleeve is 18 ¾ (19) in / 47.5 (48.5) cm long or desired length, change to smaller circular and dark gray-blue and knit 2 rnds. Now purl 4 rnds for the facing. On each purl rnd, increase 2 sts centered at underarm (M1 after first and M1 after last st). BO loosely.

FINISHING: Machine-stitch a line straight down through each of the front steek's two center stitches. Sew a vertical row of duplicate stitch over the same stitches and then carefully cut up the center between the lines. Machine-stitch straight down through the 3rd and 6th stitches of the back neck steek and cut open between the center stitches.

Lay a sleeve flat on a flat surface and measure the width of the sleeve immediately below the facing.

Mark the corresponding armhole depth on the body at the sides by hand stitching (using a contrast color thread), beginning at the center of the bound-off sts and basting straight down. Machine-stitch 2 lines from the top down on each side of the basting and then reinforce with a couple of extra stitches at the base of the armhole to prevent stitches from running. Cut the armholes open down the center of the side stitches and between the machine-

stitching. Be careful not to cut into the stitch lines. Join shoulders with three-needle bind-off or Kitchener stitch with blue-gray yarn.

Neckband: With dark blue-gray and short smaller size circular, pick up and knit sts for the neck as follows: pick up and knit 4 sts along right side of back neck, work 43 sts from back holder, pick up and knit 4 sts along left side of back neck, 25 sts along left side of front neck, work 47 sts from front holder, pick up and knit 25 sts along right side of front = 152 sts total. Work 4 rnds stockinette and, *at the same time*, decrease on every other rnd at each front neck corner as follows: mark the center st of each corner, work until 1 st before center st, slip the next 2 sts knitwise, k1, p2sso = centered double decrease. After working 4 rnds, change to malachite green and work 1 rnd without deceasing; on the next rnd, decrease at the corners as before. Now work 1 eyelet rnd for the foldline. Change to dark blue-gray and knit 7 rows; *at the same time*, increase 1 st on each side of the front corner sts on every other rnd. BO loosely.

Sew down front neck steeks to WS with small loose stitches. Trim the back neck steeks to 3-st width (including edge st), and sew down to WS with a loose row of cross stitches. Attach sleeves; fold facing down over cut stitches and sew firmly to inside of body with small loose stitches. Weave in all ends and lightly steam press under a damp pressing cloth.

Norrsunda
Arch Panel Vest

The central panel on the Norrsunda church Arch Panel vest was inspired by a painted motif in Norrsunda church that embellishes arch ribs as well as other places. The motif is a heart-shaped vine framing orange, iron oxide red, and blue-gray leaves. I decided to interpret the motif in cable knitting, with the leaves worked in a variation of intarsia knitting so that the background color can strand on the wrong side of the pattern sections.

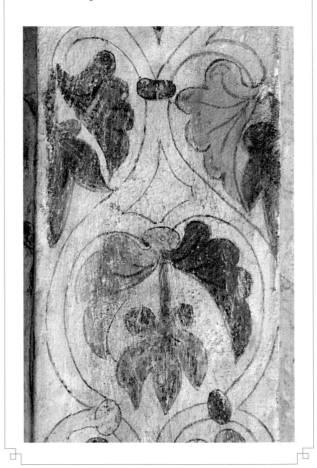

Vest

SIZES: M (L)

FINISHED MEASUREMENTS:

Chest approx. 40 ¼ (44) in / 102 (112) cm

Length: approx. 21 ¾ (22) in / 55 (56) cm

YARN: Kampes 2-ply (100% wool; 328 yd / 300 m, 100 g) Sport or equivalent.

YARN AMOUNTS:

White (natural white) approx. 230 (250) g

Orange heather 232 approx. 20 (20) g

Dark blue-gray 242 approx. 20 (20) g

Red-brown 204 approx. 10 (10) g

NEEDLES: U.S. sizes 1-2 and 2-3 / 2.5 and 3 mm: straights; 16 in / 40 cm circular U.S. size 1-2 / 2.5 mm; cable needle.

GAUGE: 25 sts and 38 rows in moss st on larger needles = 4 x 4 in / 10 x 10 cm.

Adjust needle sizes to obtain gauge if necessary.

KNITTING TIPS: Begin by reading completely through the instructions. Knit a gauge swatch to make sure you are working at the correct gauge. See "Intarsia" on page 121 (under Knitting Techniques) for information about intarsia and cable knitting. Depending on which row of the chart you are working, the increases and decreases in the cable pattern in the central panel will affect the total stitch count (also before the binding off for the armholes and neck), so that number will not be consistent throughout.

Note: If you think that intarsia is too great of a challenge, you can omit the leaf motifs and, instead, embroider them with duplicate stitch afterwards.

CHART KEY

☐ knit on RS; purl on WS.

⊟ purl on RS, knit on WS.

☐ no stitch (because of decreases in the pattern)

Ⓥ k1tbl, k1 in the same stitch; insert the left needle through the back of the vertical strand between the two sts just worked and k1 through the loop = 3 sts worked into the same st.

Ⓥ p1, yo, p1 in the same st = 3 sts worked into the same st.

Ⓐ sl 1 knitwise, k2tog, psso.

Ⓐ sl 3 knitwise, one at a time with yarn held behind, *sl the second st on the right needle over the st to the left (center st), sl the center st back on the left needle and slip the next st on the left needle over the center st **; sl the center st back onto right needle and repeat from * - ** once, purl the center st.

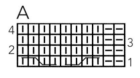 place 2 sts on cable needle and hold in back of work, k2, k2 from cable needle.

place 2 sts on cable needle and hold in front of work, k2, k2 from cable needle.

place 1 st on cable needle and hold in back of work, k2, p1 from cable needle.

place 2 sts on cable needle and hold in front of work, p1, k2 from cable needle.

place 2 sts on cable needle and hold in back of work, k2, p2, from cable needle.

place 2 sts on cable needle and hold in front of work, p2, k2 from cable needle.

place 3 sts on cable needle and hold in back of work, k2, p2tog and then p1 from cable needle.

place 2 sts on a cable needle and hold in front of work, p1, p2tog, k1 from cable needle.

■ orange heather; knit on RS and purl on WS.

■ red-brown; knit on RS and purl on WS.

■ dark blue-gray; knit on RS and purl on WS.

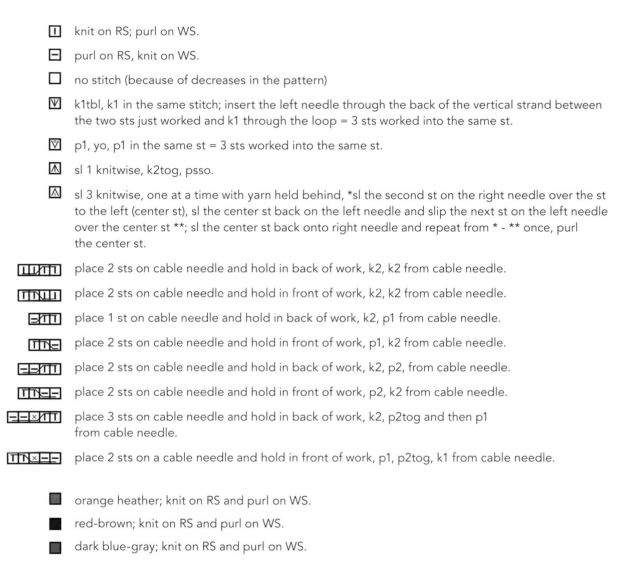

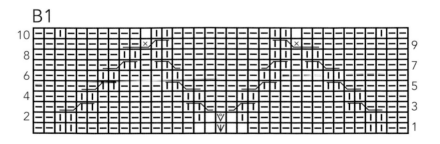

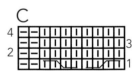

A

C

B1

B2

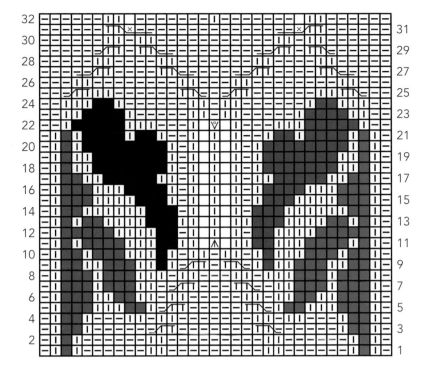

B3

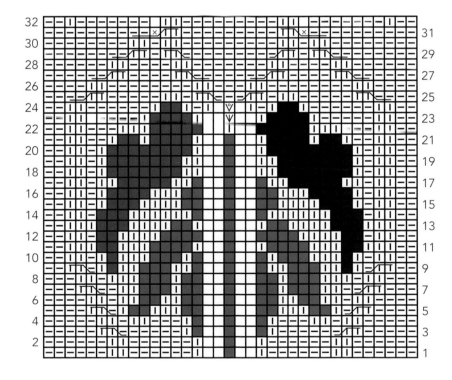

B4

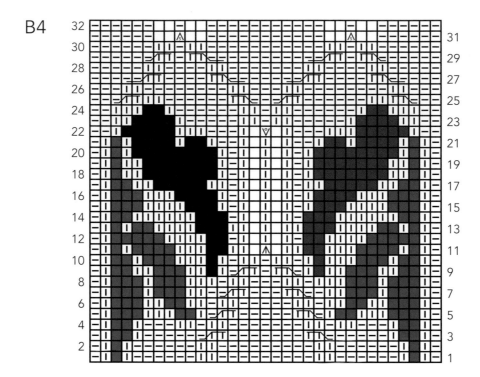

MOSS STITCH
Row 1: *K1, p1; rep from *.
Row 2: *P1, k1; rep from *.
Row 3: Work as for Row 2.
Row 4: Work as for Row 1.

BACK: With dark blue-gray and smaller needles, CO 122 (134) sts. Change to orange heather and work in k2, p2 rib for 2 rows. Change to white and continue in k2, p2 rib for another 18 (20 rows. On the last row, increase 21 sts as follows: work 2 (6) sts, M1, work 5 (7) sts, M1, *work 6 sts, M1; rep from * 18 times, work 5 (7) sts, M1, work 2 (6) sts = 143 (155) sts total. Change to larger needles and set up pattern as follows: K1 (edge st), work in moss st over 45 (51) sts, work right side cable following chart A, center cable following chart B1, left side cable following chart C, moss st over next 45 (51) sts, and end with k1 (edge st). Always knit the edge sts on every row. Continue in charted patterns as set. The intarsia cable in the center is worked in this sequence: chart B1, B2, B3, B2, B3, and B4. After a total of 104 rows in cable knitting, on row 105 (= Row 31 on chart B2 when worked the second time), BO 11 sts at each side for arm-

holes. Next BO 1 st at each side on every other row 7 (9) times. Continue without further shaping until center cable is completed.

On the row after chart B4 is completed, purl the remaining sts of center cable and, *at the same time*, decrease 4 sts over the center cable as follows: P2, p2tog, p3, p2tog, p7, p2tog, p3, p2tog, p2 = 21 sts remain over center cable. Continue in moss stitch and cables as before for 7 rows, purling the sts over the center cable. On the next row, join the side cables: work in moss st as before, p2, k1, k2tog, k2, k2tog, k1, p23, k1, k2tog, k2, k2tog, k1, p2, work moss st to end of row. On the next (WS) row, work moss st as set, work 28 (32) sts, place next 39 sts on a holder for back neck; place remaining sts on an extra needle. Turn and work each side of back separately. On every other row, at neck edge, BO 2,1,1,1 (2,2,1,1) sts. Continue working without shaping for another 2 (4) rows. Place sts on a holder. Work the other side the same way, reversing shaping and ending on a WS row.

FRONT: Work as for back but begin the moss st at the sides starting with Rows 3 and 4, followed by Rows 1 and 2. Work up to and including the

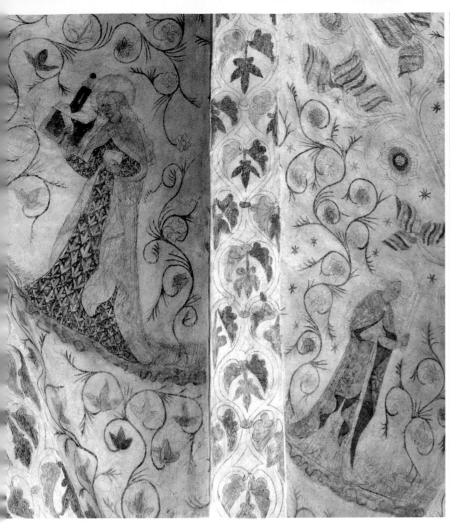

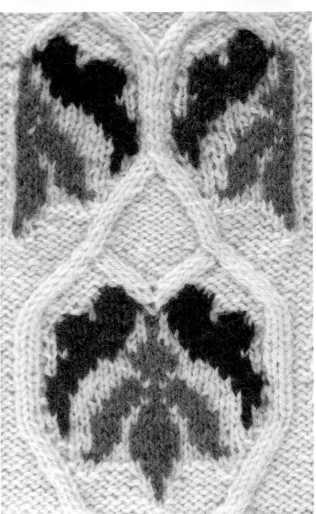

decreases over the intarsia cable. Purl 1 row after the decreases over the center cable. On the next row: work in moss st as before, p2, place next 2 sts on cable needle and hold in back of work, k2, k2tog from cable needle, k1, k2tog, k1, p23, k1, k2tog, k1, place 2 sts on cable needle and hold in front, k2tog, k2 from cable needle, p2, work in moss st to end of row.

Work 33 (37) sts, place the next 29 sts on a holder and put remaining sts on an extra needle. Turn and work each side of neck separately. At neck edge on every other row, BO 3,2,2,1,1,1 (3,2,2,2,1,1) sts. Continue without further shaping until front is same length as back. Place sts on a holder. Work the other side the same way, reversing shaping.

FINISHING: Weave in all ends on WS. Join shoulders with three-needle bind-off or Kitchener stitch. With WS facing, hand-sew the side seams with back stitch, stitching inside the edge sts. With white and smaller circular, pick up and knit sts for the neckband as follows: pick up and knit 10 (11) sts along right side of back neck, work 39 sts from back holder, pick up and knit 10 (11) sts along left side of back neck, 18 (19) sts along right side of front neck, work 29 sts from front holder, pick up and knit 18 (19) sts along left side of front neck = 124 (128) sts total. With white, work around in k2, p2 rib for 4 rnds, work 2 rnds with orange heather, and then 1 rnd with dark blue-gray. BO in rib with dark blue-gray.

Armhole bands: With white and smaller circular, pick up and knit 10 sts from the bound-off sts to the left of the side seam, 140 (144) sts around the armhole and 10 sts from the bound-off edge to the right of the side seam = 160 (164) sts total. With white, work around in k2, p2 rib for 4 rnds, then work 2 rnds with orange heather and 1 rnd with dark blue-gray. BO in rib with dark blue-gray yarn. Lightly steam press vest – except for the cables and ribbing – under a damp pressing cloth. If necessary, use white yarn to sew a few stitches (invisibly on the RS) to hold the straight center section of charts B2 and B4 together because that part of the cable might stick out too far to the sides.

Villberga
Grapevine Half Gloves

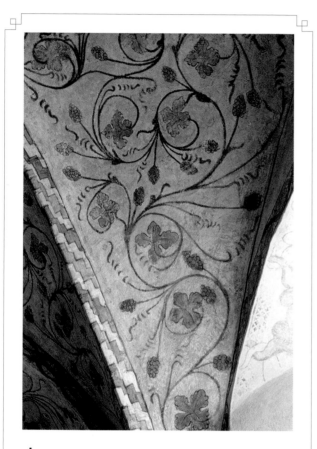

The design of the Grapevine half gloves was inspired by a richly painted roof vault in Villberga church. The ribs of the vault are beautifully decorated in various patterns painted with green and iron oxide red. A feather pattern from one of the arches has been transformed into a cable panel around the wrist of the gloves. I had the most difficulty in adapting the graceful swirling vines for two-color pattern knitting so I compromised and embroidered them on instead.

Half Gloves

SIZES: Women's S (M /L)

FINISHED MEASUREMENTS:
The gloves are approx. 6 ¾ (7) in / 17 (18) cm long and 4 (4 ¼) in / 10 (11) cm wide.

YARN: Kampes 2-ply (100% wool; 328 yd / 300 m, 100 g) Sport weight or equivalent.

YARN AMOUNTS:
White (natural white) approx. 25 (30) g
Beige 226 approx. 10 (15) g
Red-brown 204 approx. 5 (5) g
Green heather 234 approx. 5 (5) g

NEEDLES: U.S. sizes 1-2 and 2-3 / 2.5 and 3 mm: set of 4 or 5 dpn.

EMBROIDERY THREAD: small amounts of embroidery thread, such as DMC Mouliné special in colors 3826 (burnt orange), 3853 (orange), 918 (red-brown) and 469 (leaf green).

GAUGE: 28 sts and 32 rows in charted pattern over back of hand on larger needles = 4 x 4 in / 10 x 10 cm.
Adjust needle sizes to obtain gauge if necessary.

KNITTING TIPS: Begin by reading completely through the instructions. Knit a gauge swatch to make sure you are working at the correct gauge. The embroidery is worked in chain stitch as shown in the photos, with 3 strands DMC Mouliné or a similar embroidery thread.

Note: For a simpler version of the half-gloves, omit the individual fingers. Instead, follow the instructions until charted pattern is complete and then continue with white yarn and smaller needles: work 2 rnds in stockinette and end with 2 rnds k1, p1 rib. BO loosely in rib.

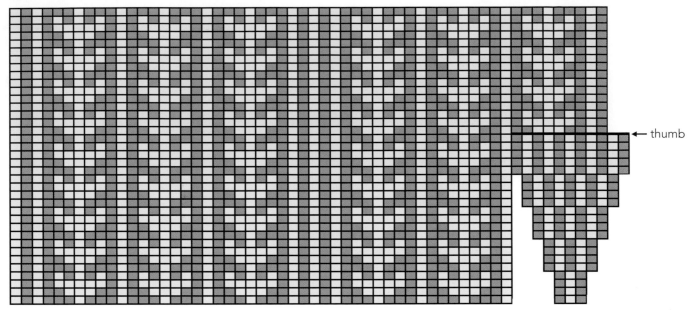

← thumb

□ white
■ beige

RIGHT GLOVE: With white and smaller dpn, CO 48 (56) sts. Join, being careful not to twist cast-on row. Begin with double moss stitch:
Rnd 1: K2, p2.
Rnd 2: Work as for Rnd 1.
Rnd 3: P2, k2.
Rnd 4: Work as for Rnd 3.

Repeat these 4 rnds once = a total of 8 rnds. Cut yarn. Knit the next round (set-up round for braid), alternating 1 st each red-brown and green heather. Bring both colors to the RS, and then bring the red-brown strand over the green heather (half twisting the yarns) and p1. Bring the green heather over the red-brown and p1. Continue the same way around, changing colors on every stitch. Work the next round the same way, but bring the new yarn *under* the old one. Now change to white and knit 1 rnd.

Change to larger dpn and work in pattern following chart A for size S and chart B for size M/L. *Note:* When working the first rnd of the chart, increase 1 st (with M1) at the beginning and 1 st in the center of the rnd = 50 (58) sts. The increases on each side of the thumb gusset are made with M1 (lift strand between two stitches with left needle and knit into back loop). At the arrow for the thumb on the chart, place the first 11 (13) sts of the round on a holder. CO 9 (11) sts and continue following chart. After completing charted rows, continue with smaller dpn and white. On the next rnd, work 21 (24) sts, place the next 13 (15) sts on a holder for the little finger, CO 1 st and complete rnd. Work another 2 rnds on remaining sts. *Index finger:* work 7 (8) sts (from inside of glove), place the following 29 (33) sts on a holder, CO 1 st and continue on the remaining 8 (9) sts of rnd (from outside of glove) = 16 (18) sts. Work 2 rnds in stockinette and then 2 rnds k1, p1 rib. BO loosely in rib. *Middle finger:* Work the first 7 (8) sts from the last sts set aside (inside of glove), CO 1 st and work the last 7 (8) saved sts (from outside of glove), finish the first rnd by picking up and knitting 1 st at base of index finger = 16 (18) sts. Work 2 rnds in stockinette and then 2 rnds k1, p1 rib. BO loosely in rib. *Ring finger:* Work the remaining 15 (17) sts from holder and pick up and knit 1 st at base of middle finger = 16 (18) sts. Work 2 rnds in stocki-

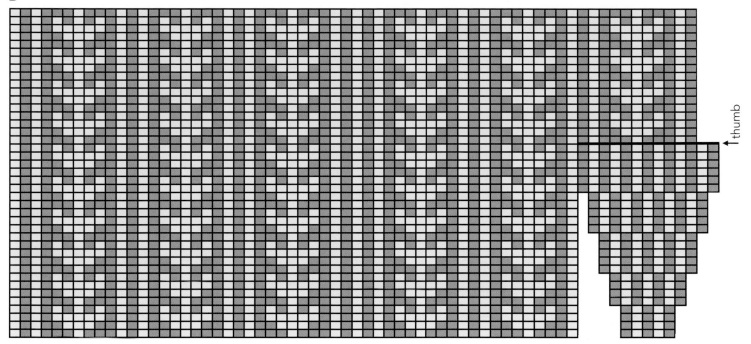

thumb

nette and then 2 rnds k1, p1 rib. BO loosely in rib as for other fingers. *Little finger:* Work the 13 (15) sts set aside for little finger and pick up and knit 1 st at base of ring finger – 14 (16) sts. Knit 2 rnds in stockinette and then work 2 rnds in rib as for other fingers. BO loosely in rib.

THUMB: Place thumb sts onto dpn and knit with white; pick up and knit 1 st at side of thumbhole, 11 sts across back of thumb, and 1 st on other side of thumbhole = 24 (26) sts total. Divide sts over 3 dpn and work 9 (10) rnds in stockinette and then 3 rnds k1, p1 rib. BO loosely in rib.

LEFT GLOVE: Work as for right glove, reversing shaping. Begin round at lower left side of chart and work left to right. Make sure the fingers and thumb are placed correctly!

FINISHING: Weave in all ends neatly on WS and, with white and a couple of small stitches for each, sew (as invisibly as possible) any gaps between the

fingers. Lightly steam press (except for the braid and lower edge) under a damp pressing cloth. Free-hand embroider a grapevine on the back of the hand using regular and elongated chain stitches and 3 strands DMC mouliné thread. See close-up photo of the glove on the next page as a template for the embroidery. Also see the section about embroidery on knitted fabric under Embroidery on page 125. Begin by marking the placement of the embroidery, basting the lines in a contrast color. The embroidery is approx. 21 sts wide and 22 rows long and is placed at the center of the back of the hand between chart rows 13-35 for size S and 16-38 for M/L. Use a line of chain stitches for the stems and leaf veins and single, elongated and abutting chain stitches for the leaves. The berry-like grape cluster is embroidered with a couple of round stitches, one above the other, for each grape; first make a little larger stitch with dark orange and then a smaller one with a lighter shade. Remove the basting once the embroidery is finished.

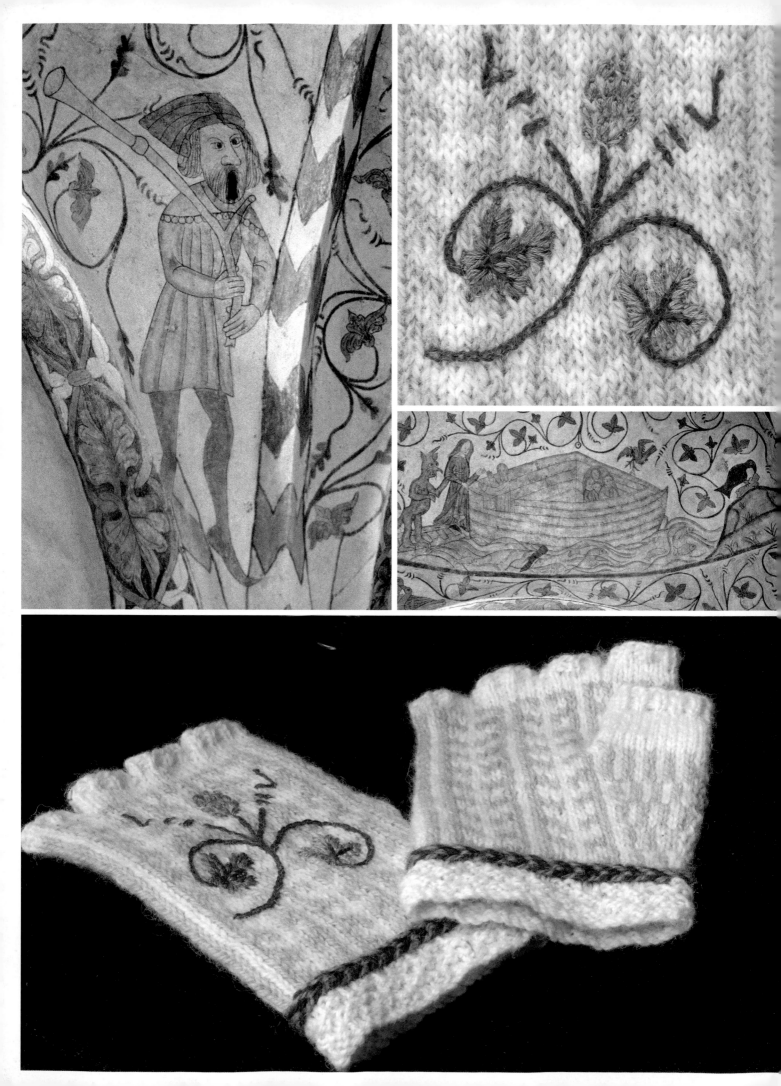

Litslena
Chevron Scarf

Some zigzag patterns on the vault ribs in Litslena church inspired this chevron scarf. The blue-green has changed over time and is now just barely visible. This is only one of the color combinations that appear in the paintings.

Scarf

SIZE: One size
Finished Measurements:
Width approx. 8 ¾ in / 22 cm; length approx. 73 in / 185 cm.
YARN: Kampes 2-ply (100% wool; 328 yd / 300 m, 100 g) Sport weight or equivalent.
YARN AMOUNTS:
White (natural white) approx. 85 g
Dark blue-gray 242 approx. 25 g
Red-brown 204 approx. 25 g
Light turquoise 244 approx. 25 g
NEEDLES: U.S. size 6 / 4 mm.
GAUGE: 24 sts and 26 rows in lace pattern = 4 x 4 in / 10 x 10 cm. Adjust needle size to obtain gauge if necessary.
KNITTING TIPS: Begin by reading completely through the instructions. Knit a gauge swatch to make sure you are working at the correct gauge.
Note: For an even easier variation, you can knit the scarf in one piece, a total of 73 in / 185 cm long. End with 4 rows white and then BO loosely on the next row. If the scarf is worked this way, the points on the bound-off edge will be the reverse of those for the cast-on.

SCARF: With white, CO 51 sts.

Row 1 (RS): *K1, yo, k3, 1 centered double decrease (sl 2 knitwise, k1, p2sso), k3, yo*; rep from * to * 5 times and end with k1.

Row 2 (WS): Knit.

Repeat Rows 1-2 a total of 3 times = 6 rows and then change colors. Work in this color sequence, with 6 rows in pattern for each color: red-brown, white, dark blue-gray, white, light turquoise, white. Repeat the stripe sequence a total of 6 times, but, on the last stripe with white, work only 4 rows. Place sts on a holder and then make another piece the same way.

FINISHING: With RS facing, join the two halves of the scarf with Kitchener stitch or, with RS facing RS, join with three-needle bind-off. Weave in all ends. Very gently steam press the scarf under a damp pressing cloth (the iron should just barely touch the pressing cloth) so that the steam seeps down through the scarf.

Tierp Group

Paintings attributed to the Tierp Group are distinguished by, among other things, the so-called sea grass ornamentation as is shown on the roof vault in this picture. The picture was taken in Sånga church and all the garments in this section of the book were inspired by the church's abundant paintings that were unfortunately damaged by previous rough restoration attempts.

Sånga
Leaf Pattern Vest

The motif that inspired this Leaf Pattern vest is a brocade-like pattern used to decorate the clothing of several figures, as for example, the garment the apostle Philip wears under his cloak. The motif appears in several color combinations and was most likely painted with stencils. It is a rather sprawling pattern that was difficult to replicate and so this is my interpretation of it. The shaping of the vest was inspired by a vest-like garment from a scene featuring Jesus on the cross.

Vest

SIZES: S (M, L)

FINISHED MEASUREMENTS:

Chest approx. 38 ¼ (40 ¼, 42 ½) in / 97 (102, 108) cm

Length: approx. 22 (23 ¼, 23 ¼) in / 56 (59, 59) cm

YARN: Kampes 2-ply (100% wool; 328 yd / 300 m, 100 g) Sport weight or equivalent.

YARN AMOUNTS:

Red-brown 204 approx. 150 (160, 170) g

Pale violet 261 approx. 120 (130, 140) g

NEEDLES: U.S. sizes 0 and 2-3 / 2 and 3 mm: 16 and 32 in circulars.

GAUGE: 28 sts and 33 rows in charted pattern on larger needles = 4 x 4 in / 10 x 10 cm.

Adjust needle sizes to obtain gauge if necessary.

KNITTING TIPS: Begin by reading completely through the instructions. Knit a gauge swatch to make sure you are working at the correct gauge.

Note: Because the steeks replace a larger number of stitches on the armholes and neck, you may need a short circular to work the top of the vest.

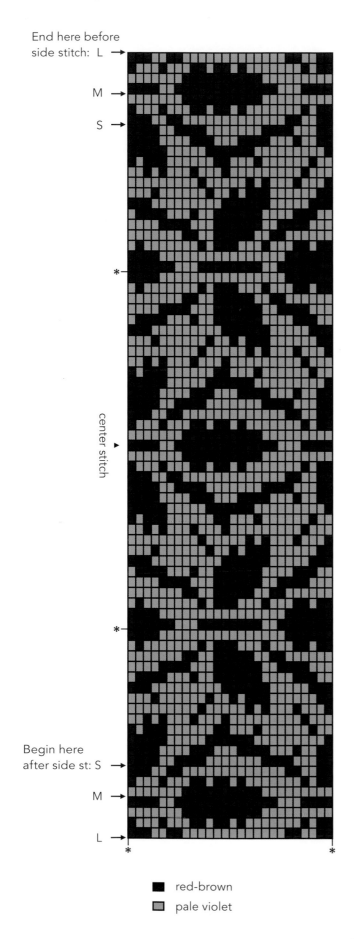

End here before
side stitch: L

M

S

*

center stitch

*

Begin here
after side st: S

M

L

*

*

■ red-brown
□ pale violet

BODY: With red-brown and smaller circular, CO 260 (272, 288) sts; join, being careful not to twist cast-on row. Place a marker between the last and first sts to indicate beginning of rnd. Purl 1 rnd, knit 1 rnd, purl 1 rnd. Place a marker after 130 (136, 144) sts. The first st of the rnd and the first st after the second marker are side sts and should always be knit with red-brown. Change to larger circular and work in pattern following the chart, beginning at arrow for your size; end before and after the side st (the chart shows half a round but not the side sts or the decreases at the sides). Work the repeat from * to * (see asterisks on left side of the chart) a total of 3 times per half rnd. Work in pattern for 8 (12, 12) rnds. On the next rnd, decrease 1 st at each side of the side sts with k2tog on the left side of the side st and ssk on the right side. Decrease the same way on every 5th (5th, 6th) rnd 6 (6, 5) times = 232 (244, 264) sts remain. Continue without shaping for 8 (8, 7) rnds. On the next rnd, increase with M1 on each side of each side st and then increase the same way on every 5th (5th, 6th) rnd 9 (9, 8) times = 272 (284, 300) sts; work new sts into pattern. Work without shaping for 15 (18, 15) rnds. Cut yarn. Place the last 9 (9, 10) sts knitted on a holder with the first 10 (10, 11) sts of rnd. CO 4 sts, work 117 (123, 129) sts, place the next 19 (19, 21) sts on a holder, CO 8 sts, work to end of rnd and CO 4 sts. The new sts form the armhole steeks. The first and last st of the steek are edge sts and are always knit with pale violet; the remaining steek sts are worked in alternating colors checkerboard fashion. Continue working in the round and begin shaping the armhole on the next rnd by decreasing 1 st outside each steek edge st: decrease with ssk on right side of steek and k2tog on left side. Decrease on every other rnd 10 (11, 13) times. Continue armhole without further shaping.

Note: On the same rnd as the 7th (on the rnd after the 7th, on the rnd after the 8th) armhole decrease, place the center 3 sts of front on a holder. CO 8 sts and work steek as for armholes. Now begin shaping front neck as follows: with k2tog on left side of neck and ssk on right side, decrease 1 st on each side of center st on the next rnd and then on every other rnd 14 (17, 17) times and on every 3rd rnd 9 (8, 8) times.

Note: On the rnd after (on the 2nd rnd after, on the 2nd rnd after) 22 (24, 24) decreases have been made for front neck, place the center 45 (49, 49) sts on back on a holder for back neck. CO 8 sts for back neck steek and work as for other steeks. Continue in pattern, shaping back neck beginning on next rnd, with k2tog on left side of neck and ssk on right side, decrease 1 st outside each steek edge st. Work another 2 rnds without decreasing. Cut pale violet and continue with red-brown only. Knit 1 rnd, binding off side sts and steeks as you work around. Place each set of shoulder sts on a separate holder.

FINISHING: Hand-stitch a line of back stitches through the center of the 2nd and 7th sts of each armhole steek. Make a vertical line of duplicate stitches over the 4th and 8th steek sts. Cut the steeks open between the duplicate stitch lines, making sure you don't cut into the stitch lines. Reinforce the front and back neck steeks the same way.

Armhole bands: With red-brown and short smaller size circular, work the last 10 (10, 11) sts on armhole holder, pick up and knit 121 (127, 131) sts around armhole and then work the last 9 (9, 10) sts from holder. Join and purl 1 rnd, knit 1 rnd, purl 1 rnd. BO knitwise, somewhat firmly.

Neckband: With red-brown and short smaller size circular, pick up and knit 8 sts along the right side of back neck, work sts from back neck holder, pick up and knit 8 sts along left side of back neck, 50 (54, 54) sts along left side of front neck, work sts from front holder, pick up and knit 50 (54, 54) sts along right side of front neck. Join and purl 1 rnd, knit 1 rnd, purl 1 rnd and, at the same time, decrease at the base of the V-neck on every rnd with p3tog on purl rnds and 1 centered double decrease (sl 2 knitwise, k1, p2sso) on the knit rnd. BO knitwise, somewhat firmly.

Sew down steeks on WS with small loose stitches. Weave in all ends. Lightly steam press vest under a damp pressing cloth.

Sånga
Carnation and French Lily Sweater

The inspiration for the Carnation and French Lily sweater is taken from a painting in Sånga church that shows St. Eskil in full bishop's attire. A carnation-like flower on the dark ground next to him was the basis for the motif in the dark stripes, and the stencil-painted French lilies on the cope provided the light motif. The colors for the sweater's lower panel come from the shoes and lower part of his costume. The stenciled motif on the lower part of the sweater derives partly from surface filler around Eskil, partly in a much newer window panel below it that was revealed in the 1902 renovation.

Sweater

SIZES: S/M (L)

FINISHED MEASUREMENTS:
Chest approx. 40 ½ (45) in / 103 (114) cm
Length: approx. 23 ¾ (24 ¾) in / 60 (63) cm
Sleeve length: approx. 19 (19 ¾) in / 48 (50) cm

YARN: Kampes 2-ply (100% wool; 328 yd / 300 m, 100 g) Sport weight or equivalent.

YARN AMOUNTS:
Black approx. 260 (310 g)
Malachite green 257 approx. 210 (260) g
Dark old rose 225 approx. 50 (50) g
Red-brown 204 approx. 50 (50) g
White (natural white) approx. 50 (50) g
Dark orange heather 228 approx. 50 (50) g

NEEDLES: U.S. sizes 1-2 and 2-3 / 2.5 and 3 mm: 16 and 32 in / 40 and 80 cm circulars + set of 4 or 5 dpn.

GAUGE: 28 sts and 32 rows in pattern following chart C or D on larger needles = 4 x 4 in / 10 x 10 cm. Adjust needle sizes to obtain gauge if necessary.

KNITTING TIPS: Begin by reading completely through the instructions. Knit a gauge swatch to make sure you are working at the correct gauge. All single-color rows are worked with the smaller needle and two-color rows with larger needle.

Note: In order to offer this sweater in two sizes, I had to arrange the pattern somewhat differently on charts C and D. The white stripes are a little more obvious on size L than for size S/M. The motif for the lower panel is also a bit more filled in for size L.

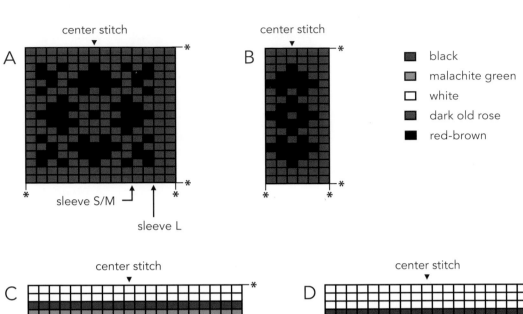

A

B

center stitch

sleeve S/M

sleeve L

black

malachite green

white

dark old rose

red-brown

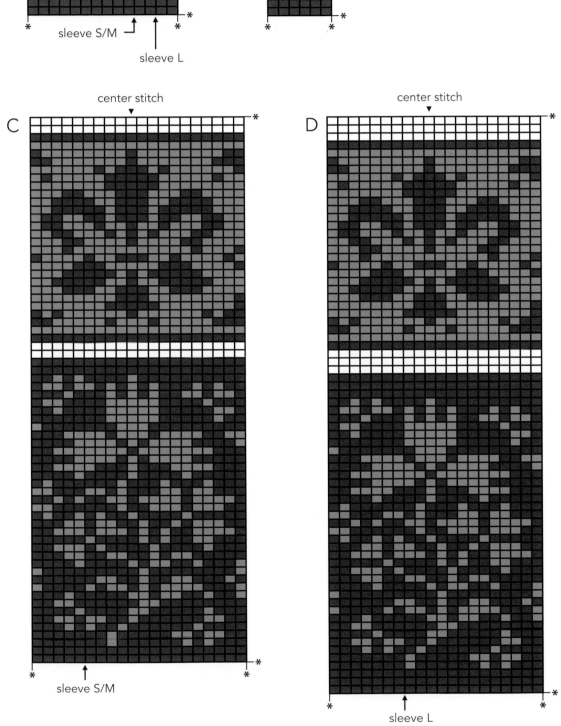

C

D

center stitch

center stitch

sleeve S/M

sleeve L

BODY: With dark orange heather and smaller circular, CO 280 (320) sts; join, being careful not to twist cast-on row. Place a marker between the last and first sts to indicate beginning of rnd. Knit 5 rnds. Work an eyelet rnd (*k2tog, yo; rep from * around) for foldline. Work another 7 rnds in stockinette. Now work in pattern following the chart – don't forget to use the smaller needle for single-color rounds and larger needle for two-color rounds. *Size S/M:* Work chart A. *Size L:* Work the last 3 sts of chart B and then chart A 11 times, chart B 1 time, chart A 11 times and end with the 3 first sts on chart B. *Both sizes:* After completing bottom panel, continue with pattern on chart C (D). Work the 68 (72) rows of charted pattern 2 times and then continue in pattern for another 12 (14) rnds. On the next rnd: work 54 (64) sts, place 33 sts on a holder for front neck, CO 10 sts for front neck steek and then complete rnd. The first and last st of the steek are edge sts and are always knit with MC; the remaining steek sts are worked in alternating colors checkerboard fashion. Continue working in the round and begin shaping the neck on the next rnd by decreasing 1 st outside each steek edge st: decrease with k2tog on right side of neck and ssk on left side. Decrease on every rnd 5 times and then on every other rnd 3 times. Work 5 (6) rnds without shaping. On the next rnd, place the center 43 sts on back on a holder. CO 10 sts for back neck steek. On the following rnd, decrease 1 st outside each back neck steek edge st and then decrease on every other rnd 2 times. Work 3 more rnds without deceasing. Change to smaller circular and red-brown and knit 1 rnd. On the next rnd: BO 1 st (side st), work 45 (55) sts, BO 10 steek sts, work 45 (55) sts, BO 1 st (side st), work 45 (55) sts, BO 10 steek sts, work 45 (55) sts. Place each set of shoulder sts on a separate holder.

SLEEVES: With dark orange heather and smaller dpn, CO 64 (68) sts. Join and work 5 rnds in stockinette. Work an eyelet rnd (*k2tog, yo; rep from * around) for foldline. Work another 6 rnds in stockinette. Work in charted pattern as for body and don't forget to use the smaller needles for single-color rounds and larger needles for two-color rounds. Begin after the first st on the round at the arrow for your size sleeve on chart A; the first st of the round is always knit with MC. On every 4th rnd, increase 2 sts at center of underarm: M1 after the first st and M1 after the last st; work new sts into pattern. Change to circular when sts fit around. The pattern repeat for chart C (D) is worked a total of 2 times in length. Continue with black and first knit 1 rnd, then purl 4 rnds for the facing. On every purl rnd, increase with M1 after the first st and M1 after the last st. BO loosely.

FINISHING: Hand-stitch a line of back stitches through the 2nd and 9th sts of the front and back steeks and cut steeks open between the center stitches. Lay a sleeve flat on a flat surface and measure the top width immediately below the facing. Mark the corresponding armhole depth on the body at the sides. With contrast color thread, hand-stitch straight down beginning at the center of the bound-off side st. Machine-stitch 2 lines on each side of the basting and reinforce at the base of the armhole with a couple of extra stitches so the stitches won't run. Cut steeks open at the center between the machine-stitched lines, making sure you don't cut into the stitch lines because the stitches might unravel. Join the shoulders with three-needle bind-off or Kitchener stitch.

Neckband: With red-brown and short smaller size circular, pick up and knit 8 sts along right side of back neck, work sts from back holder, pick up and knit 8 sts along other side of back neck, 21 sts along left side of front neck, work sts from front holder, pick up and knit 21 sts along right side of neck. Join and knit 4 rnds, purl 1 rnd for foldline and then knit 4 rnds. BO loosely. Trim the steeks to width of 3 sts and sew to WS using loose cross stitches down the steek edge. Fold in facings at lower edges and neck and sew down with small loose stitches on WS. Attach sleeves; fold facings over cut edges and sew down well to WS with small loose stitches. Weave in all ends. Lightly steam press sweater under damp pressing cloth.

Sånga
Verdigris Panel Child's Sweater

The motif for the Verdigris Panel sweater was inspired by a stenciled pattern in iron oxide red from Sånga church that was used sometimes as surface filler and sometimes in borders. When the medieval church paintings, which had been whitewashed in 1687, were (rather harshly) restored in 1902, templates for a new and somewhat larger stencil were made following the original medieval ones. This was used to paint new borders with iron oxide red around the windows, and a turquoise border inside a door arch. The entire turquoise panel was painted in precisely the same color, but now more than a century has elapsed and half of the panel's partial motifs have changed color. I don't know which color pigment was used when the panel was painted, but it is now a verdigris shade with several different blue-green shades, from lustrous turquoise to deepest sea green. The lower edge and neck-band of the child's sweater are worked in moss stitch rib. The same sweater for adults has a little shawl collar in moss rib.

Child's Sweater

SIZES: 2 (5, 8) years

FINISHED MEASUREMENTS:
Chest approx. 27 ½ (31 ½, 35 ½) in / 70 (80, 90) cm
Length: approx. 13 (17, 19 ¾) in / 33 (43, 50) cm
Sleeve length: approx. 10 ¾ (13, 15) in / 27 (33, 38) cm

YARN: Kampes 2-ply (100% wool; 328 yd / 300 m, 100 g) Sport weight or equivalent.

YARN AMOUNTS:
White (natural white) approx. 160 (210, 270) g
Light turquoise 244 approx. 30 (30, 40) g
Dark turquoise 250 approx. 30 (30, 30) g
Malachite green 257 approx. 30 (30, 40) g
Light turquoise heather 251 approx. 30 (30, 30)

NEEDLES: U.S. sizes 1-2 and 2-3 / 2.5 and 3 mm: 16 and 24 or 32 in / 40 and 60 or 80 cm circulars + set of 4 or 5 dpn. Use circular length appropriate for sweater size.

GAUGE: 28 sts and 34 rows in charted pattern on larger needles = 4 x 4 in / 10 x 10 cm.
Adjust needle sizes to obtain gauge if necessary.

KNITTING TIPS: Begin by reading completely through the instructions. Knit a gauge swatch to make sure you are working at the correct gauge. The single-color rounds are worked with smaller size needle and the two-color rounds with larger needle.

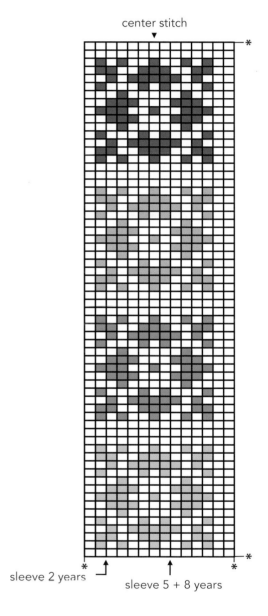

white
light turquoise
dark turquoise
malachite green
light turquoise heather

center stitch

sleeve 2 years

sleeve 5 + 8 years

MOSS STITCH RIB:

Rnd 1: *K3, p1; rep from * around.
Rnd 2: P1, *k1, p3; rep from * around and end with p2.
Repeat these 2 rnds.

BODY: With white and smaller circular, CO 188 (216, 244) sts; join, being careful not to twist cast-on row. Place a marker between the last and first sts to indicate beginning of rnd. Work around in moss stitch rib for 1 ¼ (2, 2) in / 3 (5, 5) cm. Knit 1 rnd, increasing 8 sts evenly spaced around = 196 (224, 252) sts. Now work in pattern following the chart. Don't forget to work the single-color rounds with smaller needle and two-color rounds with larger needle. Work the 64 rows of pattern repeat 1 (1, 2) times and then work another 24 (47, 7) rnds in pattern = 88 (111, 135) pattern rows. Cut yarn, skip 42 (48, 52) sts, place the next 15 (17, 23) sts on a holder. Now work back and forth in pattern (the row begins at the left side of front neck). BO 3-2-2-2 (4-2-2-2, 4-2-2-2) sts on each side of neck. Work 2 (2, 2) rows without shaping. On the next row, place the center 23 (27, 33) sts at center back on a holder. Work each side separately. Continue in pattern and decrease at back neck by binding off 3-2 (3-2, 3-2) sts. Work 1 (2, 2) rows without shaping. On the next row, work 32 (37, 41) sts, BO 1 st, work 32 (37, 41) sts. Place each set of shoulder sts on a separate holder.

SLEEVES: With white and smaller dpn, CO 40 (52, 52) sts. Join and work around in moss stitch rib for 1 ¼ (2, 2) in / 3 (5, 5) cm. Knit 1 rnd, increasing 8 sts evenly spaced around = 48 (60, 60) sts. Work charted pattern as for body, beginning after the first st of the round at the arrow for the sleeve for your size. Always knit the first st of the round with white. Don't forget to work the single-color rounds with smaller needles and two-color rounds with larger needles. *Size 2 years:* Increase 2 sts at center of underarm on every 3rd rnd (M1 after first st and M1 after last st). *Sizes 5 and 8 years:* Increase 2 sts at center of underarm on every 3rd rnd (M1 after first st and M1 after last st) 15 times and

then on every 4th rnd. *All sizes:* Work new stitches into pattern. When the sleeve measures 10 ¾ (13, 15) in / 27 (33, 38) cm or desired length: cut CC and, with smaller needles and white, knit 1 rnd and then purl 4 rnds for the facing, increasing on each purl rnd, M1 after first st and M1 after last st of rnd. BO loosely.

FINISHING: Lay one sleeve flat on a flat surface and measure the sleeve width at the top immediately below the facing. Mark the corresponding armhole depth on the body by hand-stitching, with a contrast color thread, down from the bound-off side st. Machine-stitch 2 lines on each side of the basting line and reinforce at the base of the armhole with a couple of extra stitches so the stitches won't run. Cut steek open between stitching lines. Join shoulders: with RS facing RS and white yarn, join with three-needle bind-off.

Neckband: With white and smaller circular, pick up and knit 8 sts along right side of back neck, work 23 (27, 33) sts from back holder, pick up and knit 8 sts along left side of back neck, 17 (20, 20) sts along left side of front neck, work 15 (17, 23) sts from front holder, pick up and knit 17 (20, 20) sts along right side of front neck = 88 (100, 112) sts total. Work around in moss stitch rib for appprox. ⅝ (⅝, ¾) in / 1.5 (1.5, 2) cm. BO loosely in p1, k1 rib. Attach sleeves, fold facing over cut stitches and sew down by hand on WS with small, loose stitches. Weave in all ends. Lightly steam press (except for ribbing) under a damp pressing cloth.

Sånga
Verdigris Panel Sweater

Sweater

SIZES: Women's M/L = Men's M (Women's XL = Men's L)

FINISHED MEASUREMENTS:
Chest approx. 47 ¼ (51 ¼) in / 120 (130) cm
Length: approx. 25 ¼ (26 ¼) in / 64 (66.5) cm
Sleeve length: women's approx. 19 (19 ¾) in / 48 (50.5) cm
Men's approx. 19 ¾ (21) in / 50.5 (53) cm

YARN: Kampes 2-ply (100% wool; 328 yd / 300 m, 100 g) Sport weight or equivalent.

YARN AMOUNTS:
White (natural white) approx. 390 (450) g
Light turquoise 244 approx. 70 (80) g
Dark turquoise 250 approx. 70 (80) g
Malachite green 257 approx. 70 (80) g
Light turquoise heather 251 approx. 70 (80)

NEEDLES: U.S. sizes 1-2 and 2-3 / 2.5 and 3 mm: 16 and 32 in / 40 and 80 cm circulars + set of 4 or 5 dpn. Crochet hook U.S. size A / 2 mm.

GAUGE: 28 sts and 34 rows in charted pattern on larger needles = 4 x 4 in / 10 x 10 cm.
Adjust needle sizes to obtain gauge if necessary.

KNITTING TIPS: Begin by reading completely through the instructions. Knit a gauge swatch to make sure you are working at the correct gauge. The single-color rounds are worked with smaller size needle and the two-color rounds with larger needle.

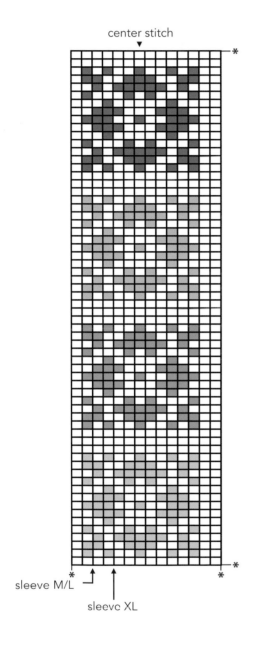

- □ white
- ▣ light turquoise
- ■ dark turquoise
- ▦ malachite green
- ▤ light turquoise heather

center stitch
▼

*

*
sleeve M/L
sleeve XL

MOSS STITCH RIB IN THE ROUND:
Rnd 1: *K3, p1; rep from * around.
Rnd 2: P1, *k1, p3; rep from * around and end with p2.
Repeat these 2 rounds.

MOSS STITCH RIB WORKED BACK AND FORTH:
Row 1: *K3, p1; rep from * across.
Row 2: K2, *p1, k3; rep from * across and end with p1, k1.
Repeat these 2 rows.

BODY: With white and smaller circular, CO 300 (312) sts; join, being careful not to twist cast-on row. Place a marker between the last and first sts to indicate beginning of rnd. Work around in moss stitch rib for 2 ½ in / 6 cm. Knit 1 rnd, increasing 36 (52) sts evenly spaced around = 336 (364) sts. Now work in pattern following the chart. Don't forget to work the single-color rounds with smaller needle and two-color rounds with larger needle. Work the 64 rows of pattern repeat 2 times and then work another 14 (17) rnds in pattern = 142 (145) pattern rows. On the next rnd, place the center front stitch on a holder = beginning of front neck. CO 8 sts for a neck steek, place markers on each side of the steek and continue working around. Work the steek alternating colors checkerboard fashion.

Note: This steek does not have edge sts. Decrease 1 st on each side of the neck outside steek markers, with k2tog on right side of neck and ssk on left. Decrease on every other rnd 13 (15) times and then on every 3rd rnd 6 times. Work without shaping for 5 rnds. Next rnd: BO 1 st (side st), work 64 (68) sts, BO 1 st (side st), work 64 (68) sts, BO 8 sts (front neck steek), work 64 (68) sts, BO 1 st (side st), complete rnd. Place front shoulder sts on holders. Divide the back sts and place the shoulder sts [64 (68) sts on opposite sides of the bound-off side sts] and the center 39 (45) sts for back neck each on separate holders.

SLEEVES: With white and smaller dpn, CO 56 (60) sts. Work in moss stitch rib for 2 in / 5 cm. Knit 1 rnd, increasing 20 sts evenly spaced around = 76 (80) sts. Now work in pattern following the chart. Always knit the first st of the round with white. Don't forget to work the single-color rounds with smaller needle and two-color rounds with larger needle. Increase 2 sts at center of underarm on every 4th rnd (M1 after first st and M1 after last st). Work new sts into pattern and change to circular when stitches fit around. Work until sleeve measures 19 (19 ¾) in / 48 (50.5) cm for women's size and 19 ¾ (21) in / 50.5 (53) cm for men or desired length. Cut CC and, with smaller needles and white, knit 1 rnd and then purl 4 rnds for the facing, increasing on each purl rnd, with M1 after first st and M1 after last st of rnd. BO loosely.

FINISHING: Hand-stitch a line of back stitches down through the 1st and 8th stitches of the neck steek and then cut the steek open between the center stitches. Lay one sleeve flat on a flat surface and measure the sleeve width at the top immediately below the facing. Mark the corresponding armhole depth on the body by hand-stitching with a contrast color thread, down from the bound-off side st. Machine-stitch 2 lines on each side of the basting line and reinforce at the base of the armhole with a couple of extra stitches so the stitches won't run. Cut steek open between stitching lines. Join shoulders: with RS facing RS and with white, join with three-needle bind-off. Place the 39 (45) sts of center back on smaller circular and, with white, work back and forth in moss stitch rib as before, but on right and wrong sides. At the end of every RS row, pick up 2 sts from the edge of the front V-neck. The stitches are picked up in the pattern knitted sts that are nearest and just outside the steek, including the decreased sts. Turn and work back. Turn again and, using a crochet hook, pick up (on RS) 2 sts to the right of those worked last. Work back over the whole row (including the 2 newly picked up sts). Repeat the last 2 rows and add 2 sts at the end of every row. On the next row, skip an edge st on the neck before picking up 2 new sts and do the same at the end of the following row. Continue picking up 2 sts at the end of every row 4 times and skipping the 5th edge st. Work the new sts into rib pattern. Work this way down to the point of the V-neck. When you get to the saved st at base of V-neck and you've worked once from each direction, continue working in the round past the center st and then BO all sts loosely.

Trim the neck steek sts to 3 sts wide and sew down on WS with loose cross stitches down the length. Attach sleeves, fold down facings over cut edges and sew down on WS with small, loose stitches. Weave in all ends. Lightly steam press (except for ribbing) under a damp pressing cloth.

Sånga
Brocade Flower Jacket

The motif repeated over the Brocade Flower Jacket has a very brocade-like effect that was also evident in the stencilled motif that appears in garments worn by some of the biblical figures, and which inspired the jacket. The motif occurs in a variety of color combinations in several places in the church's paintings. For example, one of the apostles is illustrated wearing a cope-like garment patterned in gray blue and dark blue, a color combination I was immediately drawn to. The apostle's red-brown inner garment inspired the color for the edgings.

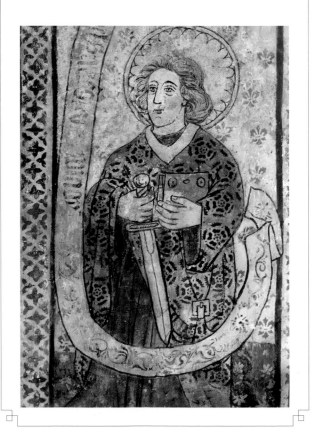

Jacket

SIZE: S/M (M/L)

FINISHED MEASUREMENTS:
Chest approx. 40 ½ (42 ½) in / 103 (108) cm
Length: approx. 24 (25 ½) in / 61 (65) cm
Sleeve length: approx. 19 ¼ (19 ¾) in / 49 (50) cm

YARN: Kampes 2-ply (100% wool; 328 yd / 300 m, 100 g) Sport weight or equivalent.

YARN AMOUNTS:
Red-brown 204 approx. 30 (30) g
Gray-blue heather 238 approx. 300 (330) g
Dark blue 224 approx. 220 (240) g

NEEDLES: U.S. sizes 0 and 2-3 / 2 and 3 mm: 16 and 32 in / 40 and 80 cm circulars + set of 4 or 5 dpn.

NOTIONS: 16 small pewter colored (or real pewter) ball buttons, approx. ¼ in / 5 mm diameter.

GAUGE: 28 sts and 32 rows in pattern following chart A1 on larger needles = 4 x 4 in / 10 x 10 cm. Adjust needle sizes to obtain gauge if necessary.

KNITTING TIPS: Begin by reading completely through the instructions. Knit a gauge swatch to make sure you are working at the correct gauge. The stitches for the sleeves are picked up around the armholes and the sleeves are worked from the top down. *Note:* If you use real pewter buttons you will need to reinforce the front band under the buttons with a rep woven band or similar type of band.

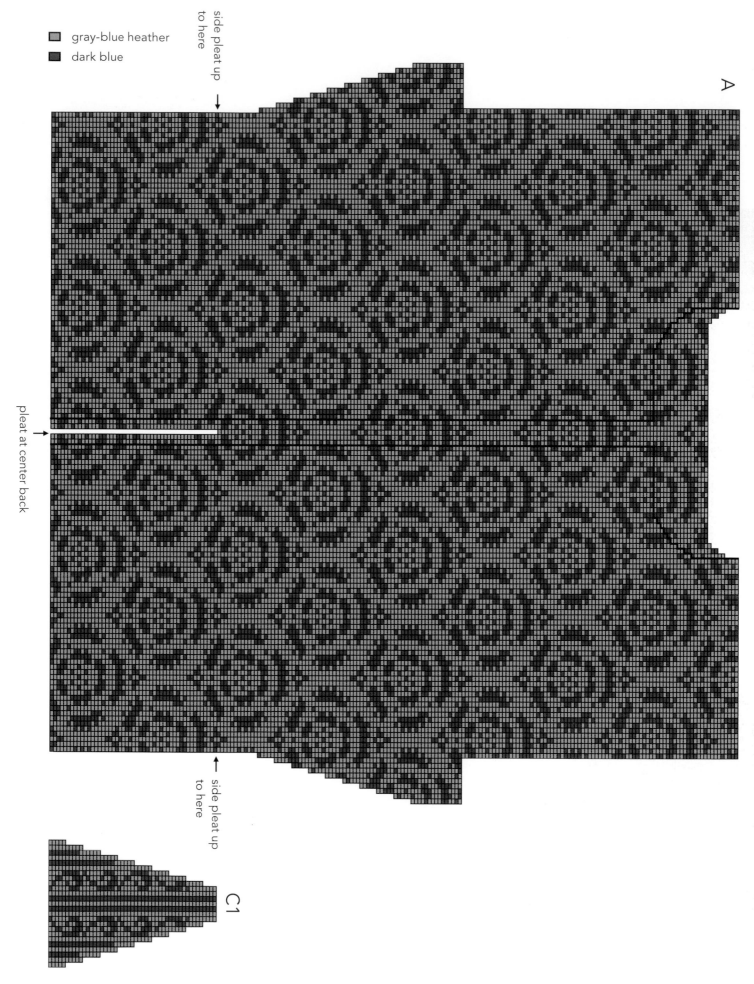

gray-blue heather

dark blue

side pleat up
to here

A

pleat at center back

side pleat up
to here

C1

C2

side pleat up
to here

pleat at center back

B

side pleat up
to here

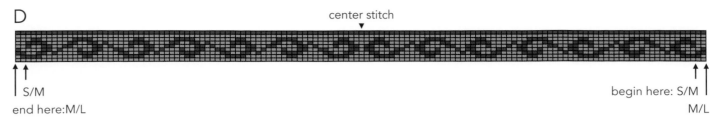

center stitch
▼

↑↑   ↑↑
↑   ↑
S/M   begin here: S/M
end here:M/L   M/L

E center stitch
▼

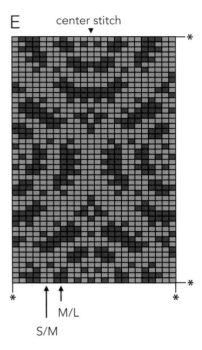

*M/L
S/M

BODY: With red-brown and smaller circular, CO 319 (345) sts. Work back and forth for 4 rows as follows:

Rows 1 and 3: P60 (65), k1, p23 (25), k1, p62 (67), k1, p23 (25), k1, p62 (67), k1, p23 (25), k1, p60 (65).

Rows 2 and 4: Purl.

Cut yarn. Change to larger circular and, with grey-blue heather, CO 5 sts; join, being careful not to twist sts. Work around in pattern, following chart A (B), and chart C1 (C2) where indicated on the larger charts for the pleats (sides and center back); end the rnd by casting on 5 sts. The first 5 and last 5 sts of the round are the steek sts that should be worked as follows: the first and last sts in the steek are edge sts that are always knit with MC; the remaining sts are alternately knit with MC and CC checkerboard fashion. Work following the chart for a total of 49 (54) rnds. Shape the pleats with 1 ssk on the right side and k2tog on the left side of the pleat. Complete pleat and, on the next rnd, join the remaining pleat sts with the body sts as follows: work 57 (62) sts, place the next 3 sts

on a cable needle, hold cable needle in front of left needle and knit the sts on the cable needle together with the three first sts on left needle (in pattern following the chart), work 1 st with gray-blue heather (= side st), place the next 3 sts on a cable needle and hold behind left needle, knit the sts on the cable together with the next 3 sts on left needle (in pattern following the chart). Continue working around in the charted pattern. The center st of each side pleat is now the side st of the body which should always be knit with gray-blue heather. The center stitch of the pleat at center back continues on chart A (B) and is the center back stitch.

Work in pattern following the chart without further shaping for 11 (8) rnds.

On the next rnd: increase with M1 on each side of each side st and then increase the same way on every 5th (6th) rnd another 9 (8) times = 297 (313) sts total; work new sts into charted pattern. After completing increases, work without shaping for 14 (12) rnds. On the next rnd, work 66 (71) sts, place the next 17 sts (last 8 sts of right front + side st + first 8 sts of back) on a holder, CO 8 sts, work

127 (137) sts, place the next 17 sts (last 8 sts of back, + side st + first 8 sts of left front) on a holder, CO 8 sts, and complete rnd. The new sts form the armhole steeks that are worked as for the steek at center front (the first and last sts of the steek are edge sts). Continue around without shaping for 54 (55) rnds. Next rnd: BO the first 5 sts of rnd (steek sts), work 265 (285) sts, BO the last 5 sts of rnd; cut yarn. Place the first 14 (15) sts of rnd on a holder; with gray-blue heather, CO 4 sts, work to the last 14 (15) sts of rnd and place these sts on a holder; CO 4 sts. The new sts form the front neck steek which is worked as for the other steeks. Continue around in charted pattern and, on the next rnd, decrease 1 st on each side of the neck steek: k2tog on the right side of the neck and ssk on the left side. Decrease the same way on the next and every following rnd a total of 5 times and then decrease on every other rnd 3 times. Work without shaping for 4 (5) rnds. On the next rnd, place the center 43 (45) sts of back on a holder and CO 8 sts for the back neck steek; complete rnd. On the next rnd, decrease 1 st on each side of the back neck as for front neck. Decrease the same way on every other rnd another 2 times. Work 3 more rnds in pattern without shaping. Cut dark blue and then, with gray-blue heather, knit 1 rnd (not too loosely), binding off all steek sts at the same time. Place each set of shoulder sts on a separate holder.

SLEEVES: Hand-stitch a line of back stitches from the top down through the 2nd and 7th sts in each steek (except for the center front steek because it has 10 sts: stitch through the 2nd and 9th sts on it). Cut the steeks open at the center of the center stitches. Join shoulders with three-needle bind-off or Kitchener stitch and gray-blue heather. With larger size short circular and dark blue, beginning at the base of armhole on the side of the back armhole, pick up and knit 131 (135) sts around the right armhole, inserting needle through the edge sts of the armhole steek. Work back and forth in pattern following chart D for 9 rows, beginning at arrow for your size. Next row: with gray-blue heather, CO 1 stand then knit around. Continue in the round, following pattern on chart E (beginning at arrow for your size); the first st of every rnd should be knit with gray-blue heather. On the 4th rnd, decrease 1 st (with k2tog on left side and ssk on right side) on each side of the first st of rnd. Change to dpn when sts no longer fit around circular. Decrease a total of 32 times = 68 (72) sts remain. Continue without further shaping for another 25 (28) rnds. Change to smaller dpn and red-brown; work in garter st:
Rnds 1 and 3: Knit.
Rnds 2 and 4: Purl.
BO knitwise.

Work the left sleeve the same way, but begin picking up sts at the front. Join the underarm sts on holder with underarm of sleeve using Kitchener stitch.

FINISHING: *Neckband:* With smaller circular and red-brown, work 14 (15) sts from left front holder, pick up and knit 21 (22) sts along left side of neck, pick up and knit 9 sts along right side of back neck, work 43 (45) sts from back holder, pick up and knit 9 sts along left side of back neck, pick up and knit 21 (22) sts along right side of neck, work remaining 14 (15) sts on front holder = 131 (137) sts total. Turn and work back and forth in garter st for 3 rows. BO knitwise, a bit firmly, on RS.
Front bands: With smaller circular and red-brown, pick up and knit 140 (143) sts along left front edge, beginning at the neck by picking up sts over the edge of neckband. Turn and work in garter st for 3 rows. BO knitwise, rather firmly, on RS.

Pick up and knit 140 (143) sts along right front edge, beginning at lower edge and ending at top of neckband; turn and knit 1 row. On the next row (RS): K2 (4), BO 1 st, *k8, BO 1; rep from * 15 times; k2 (3). Next row: CO 1 st over each gap on previous row. BO knitwise, rather firmly, on RS.

Trim all the steeks to width of 4 sts (including the edge sts) and sew to WS using a loose row of cross stitches. Reinforce the buttonholes with fine stitches over the edge, all around the hole. Use thread or a finer yarn the same color as the buttonhole sts. Weave in all ends. Lightly steam press the sweater under a damp pressing cloth. Press the pleats into place. Sew on buttons.

Knitting Techniques

Techniques used in this Book

This book does not include any knitting basics. The instructions assume that the reader/knitter can cast on, work knit and purl stitches, increase and decrease stitches, and bind off. The following sections are an overview of the various knitting techniques used in this book as well as descriptions of techniques needed for finishing the knitted garments.

Gauge

Every knitter holds the yarn to different degrees of tightness or looseness. When you are going to knit something, in order to be certain that it will have the correct measurements, it is important to check your gauge before beginning to knit. In order to do that, you need to knit a gauge swatch. If the gauge on the swatch is not the same as that given in the pattern, you need to change to larger or smaller needles or else your garment will be the wrong size. Knitting a gauge swatch is a basic requirement for obtaining a good final result, particularly if you want to use another yarn than that suggested in the pattern. It seems, though, that many knitters skip this step (I've almost always regretted the times I've decided not to knit a gauge swatch). A common mistake – when someone does knit a gauge swatch – is to work the swatch back and forth even when planning to knit in the round for the project. In that case, you will undoubtedly get the correct stitch width but not the length because the length of the stitch is usually a bit longer when working in the round rather than back and forth. In other words, it is important to work the swatch the same way as the instructions specify for the garment. Color pattern knitting also produces a different gauge than single-color stockinette. At the beginning of every pattern in this book, we include the knitting technique for the gauge swatch; if it is in two-color stranded knitting, we also list which chart to follow for the swatch. If the completed swatch has too many stitches in 4 in / 10 cm, change to larger needles. If the gauge swatch has too few stitches, change to smaller needles.

Here are two different methods for working gauge swatches in the round that are useful for two-color stranded knitting. Unfortunately, the yarn for the swatch can't be reused since the swatch will be cut open.

METHOD 1: Cast on as many stitches as the pattern lists for 4 in / 10 cm + at least 10 more stitches and divide onto three or four dpn. Work around for at least half as many rounds as needed for 4 in / 10 cm in length + 4-5 rounds (half of the row count = 2.5 in / 5 cm. Cut the piece open, carefully press it flat under a damp pressing cloth, and then measure the gauge.

METHOD 2: Work as many stitches and rows as for Method 1 using two dpn or a circular. Knit on the right side only and cut yarn at the end of every row. After every row, slide the stitches rightwards down the needle; repeat to desired length. Tie the yarn ends in pairs at the beginning and end of the rows. Carefully press the swatch flat under a damp pressing cloth, and then measure the gauge.

Cable cast-on

The cast-on method that I use most often is the cable cast-on. It makes a nice-looking edge on the right side and it's practical because you don't need to measure the length of yarn you need for the cast-on. You simply take the yarn, cast on as many stitches as necessary and end when there are enough stitches on the needle.

3. Insert the right needle between the stitches (to the left of the last cast-on st) and catch the yarn.

1. Make a slip knot and place it on the left needle. Insert the right needle through the loop from the left and catch the yarn.

4. Slip the new stitch to the left needle in front of the previous two stitches by inserting the left needle from the right through the stitch so that it twists to the left when it is slipped.

2. Place the new loop on the left needle in front of the previous loop = 2 stitches.

5. Continue casting on the stitches by catching the yarn between the last two stitches just made.

Color pattern knitting

There are several ways to work color patterns, such as Fair Isle, intarsia, and mosaic knitting. The technique primarily used in this book is stockinette color patterning with two or more colors of yarn but never more than two colors per row. When working color patterns this way, there are a few things to keep in mind:

CHANGING COLORS: Always change colors the same way, always bringing the pattern or contrast color under the main or background color to emphasize the pattern. One exception to this rule is in the pattern for the Härkeberga Flowery Vine vest where you change colors the opposite way. If you always change colors the same way throughout, (for example, always bringing the new color over the old color,) the yarns will twist unevenly and the knit surface will pucker. A common Fair Isle technique is to hold the contrast color in one hand and the main color in the other hand. This method is ideal for working short pattern repeats that are only a few stitches across in the motif. I always hold both

yarns in my left hand and change yarns with the thumb, index, and middle finger but each knitter should find the method that suits him or herself. In the long run, the method that feels best in your hands is the one that works best!

STRANDING: When you are knitting with alternating strands of yarn from two balls on the same row, strands of the yarn not in use form on the back of the work. Strands or floats should lie at the correct tension on the wrong side of the fabric. They should not be pulled in too tightly because that will make the surface pucker; if they are too loose, the piece will look sloppy and uneven and the pattern won't show clearly. Hold the knitted fabric nearest the tips of the needles so that it lies sufficiently well stretched and smooth on the needles as you work, particularly the fabric on the right needle. Don't crumple up the knitting in your hands!

CATCHING FLOATS: In single-color sections stretching out over more than 5 stitches, the strand not in use should be caught on the wrong side to prevent the float from becoming too long. If floats are

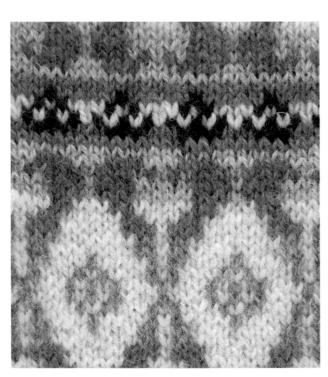

Example of two-color stranded knitting as seen on the right side (RS).

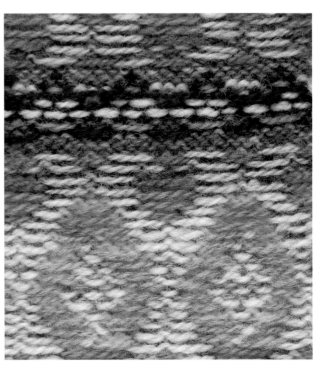

Example of two-color stranded knitting as seen on the wrong side (WS).

too long on the inside of the garment, it is easy to catch them with your fingers or something else and pull them out. That can lead to pulled and tight stitches. In the worst case, the yarn is pulled out and the stitches gape and holes form. To avoid this, you should catch the floats with the yarn in use by twisting the yarns around each other. Tug slightly at the stitches before and after the catch so that the float is not visible on the right side between them. Twist in the opposite direction the next time you catch the float so that the yarns don't twist and tangle. Avoid twisting the yarn vertically over the previous row's catch; stagger the catches sideways by at least one stitch (this is not common in two-color stranded knitting, only with catching floats). If you can't avoid twisting the floats staggered by at least one stitch sideways between the rows then twist in the same direction so that the yarn twists won't spread out each in its own direction, causing gaps where the caught yarn can show through on the right side.

BEGINNING A NEW SKEIN AND SPLICING YARN: When you've finished a skein of yarn partway through a row and you want to add a new skein of the same color, leave about 4 in / 10 cm of the old skein. Work a couple of stitches with the new skein and tie both yarn ends together with a simple knot. Do not tie a double knot! When the piece is finished, tighten the knot a bit by pulling the ends in opposite directions and then weave the ends neatly into a few stitches on the wrong side. Another useful method for joining a new skein to an old one, if they are pure wool (not machine-washable), is to splice the yarns. Divide the plies, cut about half of the strands approx. 1 ¾ - 2 in / 4-5 cm in from the end (if the yarn is two-ply, cut one of the strands). Do the same with the other yarn that will be attached to the first one. Overlap the ends and add moisture (with a little water), roll the ends quickly between the palms of your hands until they felt together and then continue knitting.

STEEKS: Steek knitting is a method usually associated with Fair Isle knitting. It's a very practical method that allows you to knit the entire body up to

Catching a float as seen from the right side of the fabric.

Catching a float as seen from the wrong side of the fabric.

Checkerboard steek with the edge stitches worked with the main color.

the shoulders in one piece and then cut the steeks. Pure wool yarn (not machine-washable) is ideal for knitting with steeks. Wool fibers catch onto each other and felt slightly, a characteristic that helps to prevent the stitches from unraveling when you cut the steek open. Other fibers (including superwash wools) can be used, but they need extra care for locking the stitches. A steek can have different

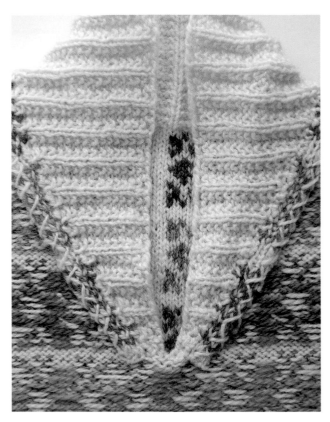

Inside of sweater with neck steek reinforced with cross stitch.

Inside of sweater with armhole steek reinforced with duplicate stitch.

numbers of stitches and be used, for example, for neck and armhole openings and the center front opening on cardigans and jackets. There are also several methods for finishing steeks. Here are two different ways that I use when I make steeks:

The first and last stitches of the steek are usually edge stitches that can be used for picking up stitches into, as on, for example, a neck, front band, or sleeve. The edge stitches are worked with the main (background) color yarn so that it is easy to see where the steek begins and ends. The other stitches in the steek are worked in alternating colors of yarn, staggering the colors so that a checkerboard pattern forms. You can also make the steeks striped if you want, with the two center stitches the same color (if the steek has an even number of stitches).

Before cutting a steek open, you have to reinforce the stitches so that they won't unravel too much as you finish the garment. One method is to hand sew a line of back stitches beginning at the bottom and working up through the center of the steek

stitches, immediately inside both edge stitches. One common method for securing the cut steek stitches against the garment's inside is to sew a line of cross stitches down the length, working in two steps over the cut edge to prevent the stitches from running. Sew down the edge with a haf cross stitch, working from the bottom up on the inside of the sweater, making sure that the stitches catch the strands from the front and back pieces. Next sew from the top down, completing each cross. It is important not to pull the stitches too tightly; otherwise, they'll form a hard ridge on the inside of the garment.

Sometimes it is more practical to machine-stitch a line from the top down through the third steek stitch (as counted inwards from each edge stitch) and then hand-sew a vertical row of duplicate stitches over the machine stitches. When you then cut the steek open at the center between the duplicate stitch lines, there is a nice edge that looks particularly good on the armhole openings on vests or for the front bands on a garment with a front opening.

Intarsia

Intarsia knitting requires working with separate small balls of yarn or long, loosely hanging strands of the pattern colors for each color field. In the intarsia variation used for the Norrsunda Arch Panel vest, the main color floats behind the work on the wrong side. The strands of the main color are caught by the pattern color yarns on the wrong side in the single-color areas that stretch over more than five stitches. A general rule is to twist the yarns around each other one stitch past each color change. If the pattern color section continues on the next row and begins vertically above or just to the right of the pattern color on the previously knit row, you should prepare the yarn change by twisting the yarns around each other one stitch ahead (on the same row it will be to the left of) of the place where you will begin using the pattern color next. You can even catch the yarn on the same row you are knitting on by twisting the main color and pattern color one stitch before the color change. The Norrsunda Arch Panel has some places in the color changes so close to each other that you can take the "rules" above with a grain of salt and twist the yarns where they are.

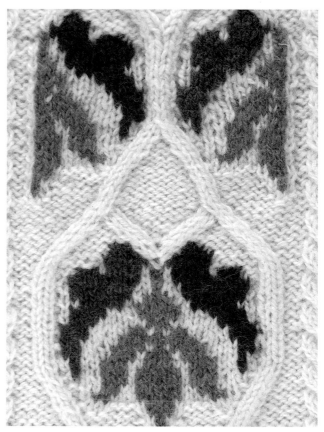

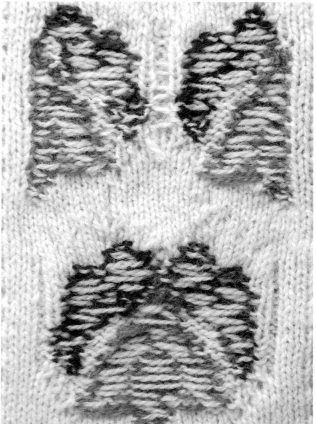

ABOVE: Detail from the center panel on the Norrsunda Arch Panel vest as seen from the right side.

The same detail as seen from the wrong side.

Cable knitting

A cable needle is used to slip and hold stitches in front or behind the work for cable knitting, to arrange the stitches in a different order and twist a group of stitches. There are many different ways of crossing the cables that can be used in different ways. Those used in the Norrsunda Arch Panel vest are described in the chart key in the pattern, so we've just included the basics of cable knitting here.

1. Crossing a cable to the right with four knit stitches: Slip two stitches purlwise to the cable needle and hold the needle behind the work, knit two stitches from the left needle and then knit the two stitches on the cable needle.

2. Crossing a cable to the left with four knit stitches: Slip two stitches purlwise to the cable needle and hold the needle in front of the work, knit two stitches from the left needle and then knit the two stitches on the cable needle.

Finishing

NORWEGIAN SLEEVE ATTACHMENT: With a few exceptions, the garments with sleeves in this book are made with the Norwegian method for attaching sleeves, with machine-reinforced cutting lines. When the body and sleeves have been completed and the neck steeks reinforced and cut open, you can measure the width of the sleeves by laying one flat on a flat surface. Measure the width at the top of the sleeve immediately below the facing. Mark

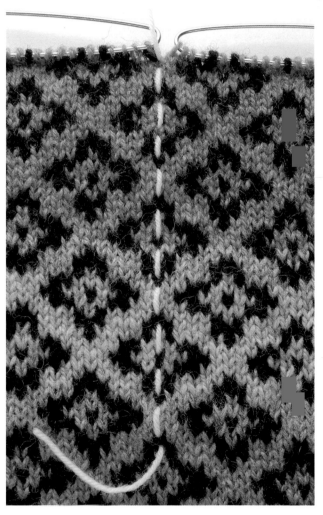

Basting the cutting line for the armhole opening.

the sleeve depth on the body at the sides by hand basting with a contrast color yarn. Sew down through the center of both side stitches if that is applicable or in the center of each side between two stitches. Next, beginning at the top and working down, machine-stitch two straight lines about one half stitch away from the basting thread. Secure at the base of the armhole with a couple of extra stitches so that the knitting won't unravel. Use sharp scissors to carefully cut the opening straight down between the stitch lines. Avoid cutting into the stitch lines because the stitches might run.

JOINING SHOULDERS: There are various ways to join shoulders on knitted garments. Here are the two methods I've used in this book.

THREE-NEEDLE BIND-OFF: Turn the garment inside out so that RS faces RS and you are working on the wrong side of the fabric. Arrange each set of stitches for a shoulder onto separate needles (dpn recommended). Hold the needles with the shoulder stitches parallel in your left hand and use a third needle and the same color yarn as for the shoulder stitches to knit the shoulders together.

1. Insert the right needle through the first stitch on the front needle and then through the first st on the back needle and knit both stitches together.

3. Pass the first knitted stitch on the right needle over the second one.

2. Knit the next two stitches together the same way.

4. Repeat steps 2-3 until all the stitches have been joined. Finish by bring the tail through the last stitch. Work the other shoulder the same way. This bind-off is firm but still flexible.

JOINING WITH KITCHENER STITCH: Place each set of stitches for a shoulder into two needles. Hold work with the right side facing you with the shoulder stitches to be joined straight across from each other. Use the same color yarn as for the shoulder stitches and a blunt tapestry needle to sew a row of duplicate stitches through the shoulder stitches. Begin by sewing through one stitch on each side; beginning with the side nearest you, and bring the needle through the first stitch and down through the first stitch on the opposite side. Next sew down through the last sewn stitch from the first side and up into the next stitch. Do the same on the opposite side. Now sew down through the last sewn stitch from the first side and up into the next stitch. Do the same on the opposite side. Drop the stitches from the needles after they have begun to be sewn together. The stitches form a new row of stitches between the sets of shoulder stitches that invisibly joins the front and back.

SLEEVES: Turn the garment inside out. Place the sleeve right side up in the body with the top edge of the sleeve at the armhole – make sure that the sleeve facing extends out – and pin baste. Make sure that the first stitch of the sleeve (center of underarm) is at the base of the armhole and the center stitch of the sleeve meets the shoulder seam. Attach sleeves by hand sewing with back stitch, working just inside the machine-stitched lines of the armhole and the purl rows on the sleeve facing. Pull the sleeve out through the armhole, pin and then sew down the facing to the inside of the body with small loose stitches.

1. Alternately sew down through the previous stitch and up through the stitch next to it...

2. ...and the same way through the corresponding stitches on the opposite side.

The sleeve facing covers the cut edges of the armhole stitches.

Embroidery on Knit Fabric

Some of the garments in this book are embellished with simple embroidery. Back stitch and duplicate stitch are worked with wool yarn on the center panel of the Härkeberga Twisted Panel. The lower panels of the Norrsunda Angel with Pillar employ simple duplicate stitch wool embroidery for the panels' flowers and leaves. The Villberga Flowery Vine half-gloves are decorated with embroidery thread chain stitches. Some of the stitches are arranged in rows one after the other and some are single round or elongated stitches next to or on each other.

Back stitch, completed and in progress.

Vertical duplicate stitch, step 1.

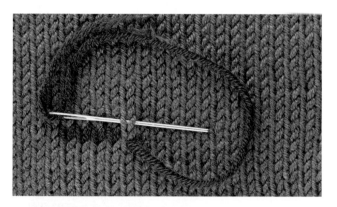

Horizontal duplicate stitch, step 1.

Vertical duplicate stitch, step 2.

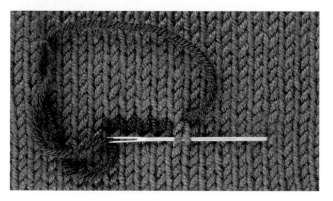

Horizontal duplicate stitch, step 2.

Chain stitch.

Making a button loop with buttonhole stitch over a yarn loop.

Button loops

First decide on how wide the loop should be and mark the placement of the loop with pins on the edge of the sweater. Attach the yarn by loosely sewing back and forth a few times between the marker pins. Use your finger to keep the strands evenly spaced. Now sew over the loops with buttonhole stitch, placing the stitches closely together until the loop is entirely covered.

Buttonholes

On garments closed with buttons, it might be necessary to reinforce the buttonholes or to join them through two layers of fabric. Using the same color thread as for the buttonhole stitches, sew around the buttonhole edge with fine stitches. If the buttonholes are small, use a finer yarn than for the knitting or a single strand from a split length of yarn.

Weaving in ends

One advantage of knitting sweaters on a circular needle in one piece up to the shoulders, using steeks and the Norwegian armhole method, is that you can avoid weaving in all the ends from the color changes at the center of the armhole or center front in the steek. These ends are simply trimmed after the armhole or steek has been reinforced. On other places, such as the sleeves, you have to weave in all the ends, and, of course, the more colors used, the more ends to weave in. Be patient and weave in one end at a time on the wrong side by sewing back and forth two or three times under some of the floats. You should sew rather loosely so that you don't pull in the stitches and make sure that the woven ends aren't visible on the right side.

Holes

Small gaps or holes can easily develop in the spaces between picked-up stitches and stitches taken from holders, as, for example, at the neck and the base of the fingers. You can sew these together with a few small stitches as invisibly as possible using yarn the same color as the stitches being closed up.

Garment care

The garments in this book are knitted with pure new wool that should be washed by hand in lukewarm water (approx. 86°F / 30°C). Use a mild wool wash (there are several no-rinse wool washes available in the U.S. and elsewhere). Do not twist or wring the garment because that could cause felting. Just squeeze lightly, rinse and then spin out the excess water (if you have a centrifuge or gentle spin cycle on your washer). Lay the fabric flat on a towel to dry. Don't wash wool garments unnecessarily. Most often just a good airing is all that's needed!

Abbreviations

BO	bind off (British: cast off)
CM	centimeter(s)
CO	cast on
DPN	double-pointed needles
G	gram(s)
IN	inch(es)
K	knit
K2TOG	knit 2 stitches together
MC	main color (background color)
M	meter(s)
M1	make 1 = lift strand between 2 sts and knit into back loop
MM	millimeter(s)
P	purl
P2SSO	pass 2 slipped stitches over
P2TOG	purl 2 stitches together
REP	repeat
RND(S)	round(s)
RS	right side
SL	slip
SSK	slip, slip, knit: slip 1 knitwise, slip 1 knitwise, knit together through back loops
ST(S)	stitch(es)
WS	wrong side
YD	yard(s)
YO	yarnover

GAUGE = British tension
STOCKINETTE = British stocking st

Yarn

All the garments in this book use 100% wool 2-ply blanket yarn from Kampes Mill Products in Mariestad, Sweden. For more information about the yarn, see their website: www.kampes.se

Substitution: Rauma Finnullgarn from Rauma Woolen Mill or Ask (= Hifa 2) from Hillesvåg Woolens. You can order these yarns in the U.S. from:
Nordic Fiber Arts
www.nordicfiberarts.com
info@nordicfiberarts.com

For errors, please visit www.kajasticks.se/errata

Bibliography

Information about the Church Paintings:

Boëthius, Ulf. *Vägvisare till kyrkorna i Stockholms län* [Guide to the Churches in Stockholm Province]. Stockholm, 1980.

Asp, Misa. *Web films about fresco paintings at Medeltidens bildvärld* [Medieval Picture World]. Home page of the History Museum, http: medeltidbild.historiska.se/medeltidbild/

Nilsén, Anna. *Program och function i senmedeltida kalkmåleri* [Programs and functions in late medieval fresco painting]. Stockholm, 1986.

A. G. Nord, K. Tronner, Å. Nisbeth, L. Göthberg. *Färgundersökningar av senmedeltida kalkmåleri. Härkeberga, Täby, Härnevi och Risinge kyrkor* [Research on colors in late medieval fresco painting]. Stockholm, 1996.

Lindgren, Mereth. *Kalkmålningarna, ur Signums svenska konsthistoria (bd 4) Den gotiska konsten* [Fresco paintings from Signum's Swedish Art History, part 4: Gothic Art]. Lund 1996.

Early Knitting in Sweden:

Winztell, Inga. *Sticka mönster. Historisk om stickning i Sverige* [Knitting Patterns: History of Knitting in Sweden]. Stockholm, 1976.

Information about the Churches:

More information about the churches can be found on their parish home pages on the internet.

Bromma parish, Märsta parish (Norrsunda) and Färingsö parish (Sånga): www.svenskakyrkan.se

Villberga parish (Härkeberga, Litslena, Löt, and Villberga church): www.kyrkanshus.nu

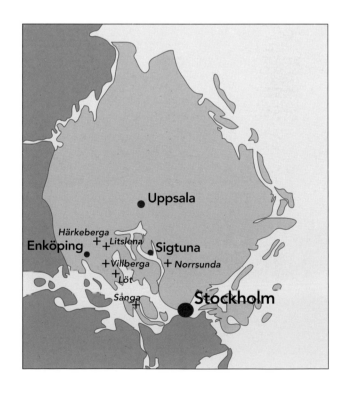

- 128 -